The Morning S

Vol. 15 JOURNAL

TEACHING

POETRY

PROPHECY

INTERCESSION

CHRONICLES

Editor: Rick Joyner
Contributing Editors: Jack Deere, Francis Frangipane, Dudley Hall
Managing Editor: Deborah Joyner Johnson
Project Manager: Dana Zondory
Layout and Design: Nicole Beals, Dana Zondory
Copy Editors: Debbie Bishop, Roger Hedgspeth, Lindsey McKay, Traci Nessler, Robin Proenneke, and Deborah Williams

The Morning Star Journal® USPS012-903 is published quarterly, 4 issues per year, by MorningStar Publications, Inc. A division of MorningStar Fellowship Church, P.O. Box 440, Wilkesboro, NC 28697. Winter 2005 issue. Periodicals postage rates paid at North Wilkesboro, NC and additional mailing offices. CPC Agreement #1472593. ISSN# 10832122

POSTMASTER: Send address corrections to *The Morning Star Journal*®, P.O. Box 440, Wilkesboro, NC 28697

Subscription rates: One year $16.95; Outside U.S. $24.95 USD.

MorningStar Publications is a non-profit organization dedicated to the promulgation of important teachings and timely prophetic messages to the church. We also attempt to promote interchange between the different streams and denominations in the body of Christ.

To receive a subscription to ***The Morning Star Journal***®, send payment along with your name and address to *MorningStar Publications*, P.O. Box 440, Wilkesboro, NC 28697, (336) 651-2400 (1-800-542-0278—Credit Card Orders Only); fax (336) 651-2430. One year (4 quarterly issues) U.S. $16.95; Outside U.S. $24.95 USD. Prices are subject to change without notice.

BIOS

Robin McMillan is currently pastoring the MorningStar Fellowship Church in Charlotte, North Carolina. With a unique preaching style, prophetic giftings, and a desire for the release of God's power, many are impacted by Robin's ministry. Robin and his wife, Donna, live in North Carolina and have four children: John Mark, Christopher, Andy, and Katy.

Mike Roberts is originally from the Charlotte, North Carolina area and has been involved at MorningStar for about ten years. He is a graduate of the MorningStar School of Ministry, and has a heart for the prophetic ministry and teaching. Mike is currently on staff at MorningStar Publications and Ministries and lives in Moravian Falls, North Carolina.

Andrew P. Surace is founder and senior pastor of Covenant Life Christian Fellowship in Seaville, New Jersey. He is a graduate of Valley Forge Christian College and has a great love for church planting. Andrew is ordained with Morningstar Ministries. He and his wife, Kathleen, have six children and five grandchildren.

Amanda Coalson is a graduate from the first year program of the Morning Star School of Ministry. She has a heart to encourage all parts of the body of Christ, especially youth. She plans to teach high school English and is an aspiring writer. Amanda and her husband, Aaron, live in Georgia.

Bob Mumford is a dynamic Bible teacher with a unique and powerful gift for imparting the Word of God. Since 1954, thousands of Christians worldwide have attributed their spiritual growth and determination to follow Jesus Christ to his prophetic teaching by helping them understand Father God and His kingdom. Bob has been a spiritual Papa to thousands of Christians, and his writings have been translated into many different languages. He seeks to bring about personal spiritual change and growth in the life of every believer. Bob can be reached at Lifechangers, P.O. Box 98088, Raleigh, NC, 27624 or call (800) 521-5676 / www.lifechangers.org.

Deborah Joyner Johnson is the managing editor of the Publications Department and oversees all publishing projects for MorningStar Publications and Ministries. She shares with her brother, Rick Joyner, a desire to see the body of Christ provided with the highest quality spiritual food that is relevant for our times. Deborah's second book, *Pathway to Purpose,* has just been released through MorningStar. She has a gifted teaching ministry and shares at conferences and women's groups. Deborah lives in North Carolina and has three children: Matthew, Meredith, and Abby.

Wade Taylor is the founder and former president of Pinecrest Bible Training Center in Salisbury Center, New York. He currently edits the quarterly publication, *The Banner.* He is the author of numerous tracts and articles and has written two books available through MorningStar, *The Secret of the Stairs* and *Waterspouts of Glory.* He travels extensively, ministering in churches and conferences.

Rick Joyner is the founder, executive director, and senior pastor of MorningStar Fellowship Church. Rick is a well-known author of more than thirty books, including, *The Torch and the Sword,* the long awaited sequel to *The Final Quest* and *The Call,* and his latest, *Delivered From Evil.* He also oversees MorningStar's School of Ministry, Fellowship of Ministries, and Fellowship of Churches. Rick and his wife, Julie, live in North Carolina with their five children: Anna, Aaryn, Amber, Ben, and Sam.

Tracee Anne Loosle is ordained with Church & Ministerial Alliance International and is the founder of Intrepid Heart Ministries. She is also a member of the MorningStar Fellowship of Ministries. Tracee's passion is to see others come into their God-given destiny. She ministers in revelatory intercession, evangelism, and teaching in the United States and abroad. Tracee and her husband, Randy, have five children.

BIOS

Steve Thompson is the associate director of MorningStar Fellowship Church, and he oversees the prophetic ministries for all of the MorningStar Fellowships. A gifted teacher and prophetic minister, Steve travels extensively throughout the United States and abroad as a conference speaker. Steve's latest book is *A 20th Century Apostle, The Life of Alfred Garr*. Steve and his wife, Angie, reside in North Carolina with their five children: Jon, Josh, Madison, Moriah, and Olivia.

Trevor Tiessen is originally from Saskatchewan, Canada. In the fall of 1996 Trevor came to Charlotte, North Carolina to attend the MorningStar School of Ministry and graduated in the spring of 1999. Since that time Trevor has been serving MorningStar Fellowship Church in the areas of church and conference administration as well as in the ministry of helps.

Dr. Morris Cerullo is the President of Morris Cerullo World Evangelism. In his more than fifty-five years of ministry, most of his time has been spent in worldwide evangelism, going to the nations preaching and teaching a powerful, uncompromised message of salvation, healing, and deliverance. He received a divine, supernatural call from God to preach at the age of fifteen. From that time until now, Morris has never wavered in his commitment and zeal to fulfill the Great Commission to bring in a harvest of souls from around the world.

Charles Haddon Spurgeon (1834-1892) was born in Essex County, England. After his dramatic conversion in 1849, he went on to preach and greatly affected the church historically through his Pastor's College. Responsible for establishing an almshouse, an orphanage, and sixty-six other institutions, Spurgeon was also an extensive and thoughtful author whose writings continue to impact the church today.

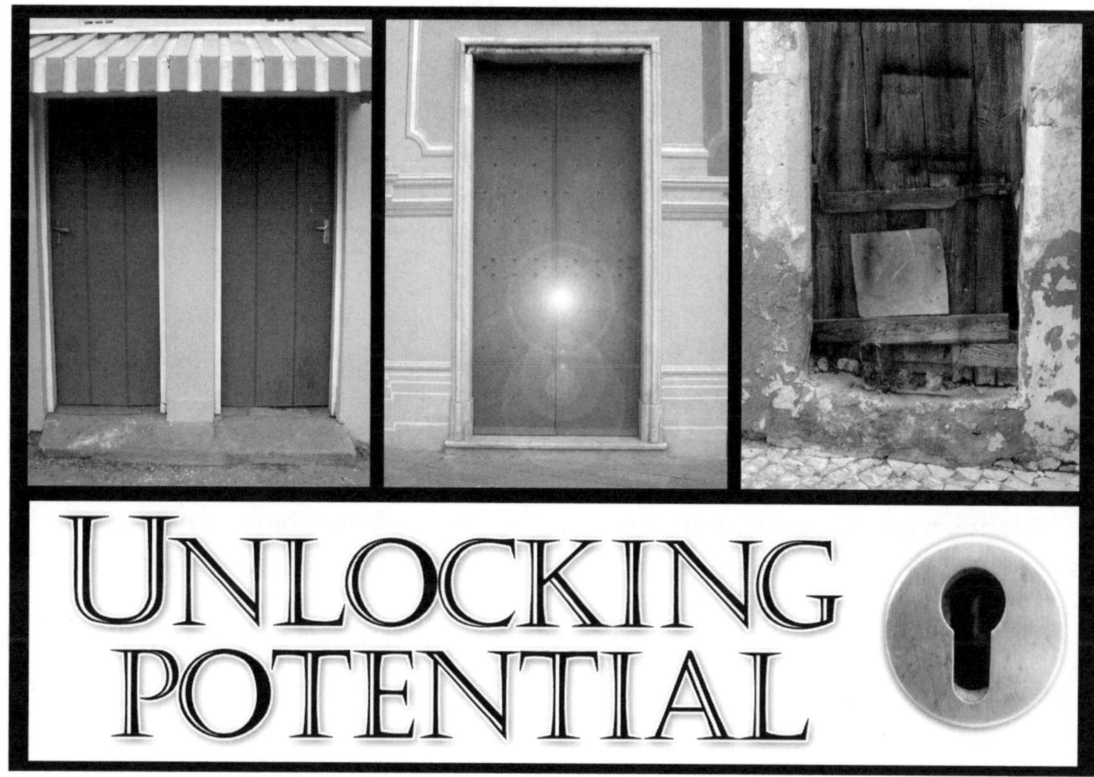

UNLOCKING POTENTIAL

All Scriptures are New King James Version unless otherwise indicated.

by Robin McMillan

As I sat in my car seeking the Lord under a large oak tree beside the Catawba River, an acorn fell through the window and landed in my lap. I picked it up and remembered an old adage: "You can count the number of acorns in an oak tree but you cannot count the number of oak trees in an acorn." Trapped inside the seed in the palm of my hand was a forest of oaks. How could its potential be unlocked?

It must be planted in the ground.

Laying Down Your Life

The process of death, burial, and resurrection is a primary method God uses to release dormant life. To be productive the acorn must be buried in the ground just like other seeds. Jesus once said;

> **"Most assuredly, I say to you, unless a grain of wheat falls into the ground and dies, it remains alone; but if it dies, it produces much grain.**
>
> **"He who loves his life will lose it, and he who hates his life in this world will keep it for eternal life" (John 12:24-25).**

Many do not bear maximum fruit because they have maintained control over their own lives, refusing to die in the spiritual sense. Jesus called this selfishness "loving your life," which imprisons the ability God has given each of us.

Identifying Your Resource

To maximize our potential we must first identify our resource. In other words,

"What is our acorn?" An example of identifying one's resource is found in II Kings 4. The wife of a former employee beseeched Elisha the prophet to help her in a very desperate situation. Her husband once served Elisha, but after his death his remaining family became indebted to creditors who threatened to enslave her sons as payment. After the prophet analyzed her situation he asked her this question:

> **... "What shall I do for you? Tell me, what do you have in the house?" And she said, "Your maidservant has nothing in the house but a jar of oil" (II Kings 4:2).**

In her estimation she had nothing valuable enough that would provide a solution to her dilemma. However, she did have a small jar of oil. Elisha knew instinctively that her small jar contained the potential to resolve all her problems.

Handling Your Resource

After identifying our resource we must discover what to do with it. The widow knew what she had, but she neither realized its potential nor how to release it. By divine revelation Elisha told her what to do:

> **Then he said, "Go, borrow vessels from everywhere, from all your neighbors—empty vessels; do not gather just a few.**
>
> **"And when you have come in, you shall shut the door behind you and your sons; then pour it into all those vessels, and set aside the full ones" (II Kings 4:3-4).**

The widow woman and her sons fully obeyed Elisha's instructions. They borrowed empty vessels from their neighbors, shut the door, and started pouring. Surely they were amazed as vessel after vessel filled to the top and overflowed. When the last empty one filled, their small jar of oil expired. Elisha told the woman to sell the oil, pay her debt, and live from the remainder. In this miraculous way God spared her family.

Overcoming Obstacles

To obey the Lord and experience His supernatural provision, we must overcome many different obstacles. One is the critical opinion of others. Other people's opinions, real and imagined, have intimidated many—enough to cause them to forsake the revealed plan of God. Some are not willing to face people's questions when no "logical" answer can be given. In the widow's case, perhaps her neighbors said, "Why would you want all of our empty vessels? You don't have anything to put in them anyway." How would she explain her request?

How do you overcome these obstacles? You simply shut the door on them.

Shutting the Door

Elisha's instructions were clear:

> **"...shut the door behind you and your sons; then pour it into all those vessels..." (II Kings 4:4).**

According to Elisha's instructions, the widow must first shut the door before pouring out her miracle. Shutting the door speaks of removing any hindrances from doing the Lord's will. Other people's opinions, our past experiences and hurts, other good ideas, and anything else that prevents us from obeying the Lord must be shut out.

Victory was not assured until the widow began pouring her small jar of oil into the first large empty container. At any point before, she could have fallen short of the plan of God and her own saving provision. She could have had all the vessels borrowed and standing in her house ready for the filling, been distracted by a neighbor's last minute opinion, and thrown down her small jar of oil in frustration. She would have missed her heavenly provision, lost her sons to slavery, and remained in a life of despair and poverty. She had to shut the door behind her.

The Door Behind

Elisha did not just tell the widow to close the door, but said **"shut the door *behind* you."** One of the most significant doors which many must close is the one that lies *behind* them, namely their past. What do you have back there that continues to plague you? Is there failure, condemnation, humiliation, loss, or even inaccurate conclusions of God's faithfulness or kindness? Shut the door behind you!

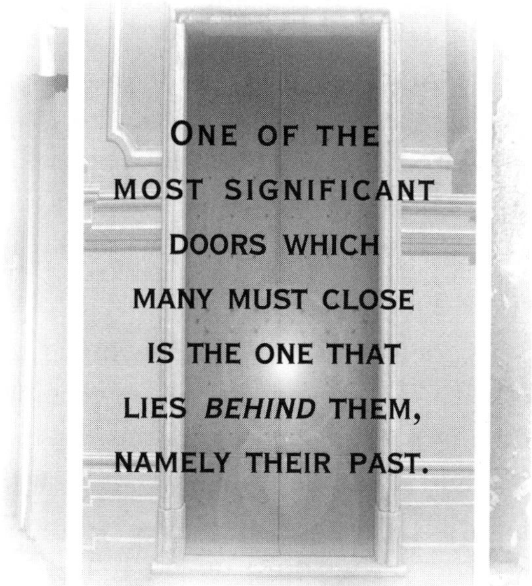

Even the greatest men of God had their own doors to shut. Jeremiah was one such man whose own conclusions about God threatened to prematurely end his effectiveness, frustrate his deliverance, and steal his destiny:

> **Therefore thus says the Lord [to Jeremiah]: If you return [and give up this mistaken tone of distrust and despair], then I will give you again a settled place of quiet and safety, and you will be My minister; and if you separate the precious from the vile [cleansing your own heart from unworthy and unwarranted suspicions concerning God's faithfulness], you shall be My mouthpiece. [But do not yield to**

them.] Let them return to you—not you to [the people].

And I will make you to this people a fortified, bronze wall; they will fight against you, but they will not prevail over you, for I am with you to save and deliver you, says the Lord.

And I will deliver you out of the hands of the wicked, and I will redeem you out of the palms of the terrible and ruthless tyrants (Jeremiah 15:19-21 AMP).

Getting Burned

A friend of mine was scheduled to minister in our regular, Friday evening training meetings. Just prior to speaking he walked through our lobby and was stopped by someone who needed to ask him a question. In our lobby we have a counter with a self-serve coffee urn. Considering the question, he backed up and leaned on the counter against the urn opening the faucet and shooting hot coffee down his backside. He scalded himself, ruined his clothes, and was obviously distracted by the episode just prior to addressing our congregation.

When he told me what happened I recognized that his experience contained a prophetic message for us all: If we back up we will get burned. Backing up is an accurate description of someone who is allowing his past to negatively affect his future. "Getting burned" is a colloquial expression that means to lose out or suffer loss. This is exactly what will happen to anyone who does not shut the door on the past.

Paul's Example

Paul the apostle knew the dangers of allowing the past to endanger the future. In his marvelous dissertation on what may separate us from the love of God in Christ Jesus, he identified a number of things over which we have victory.

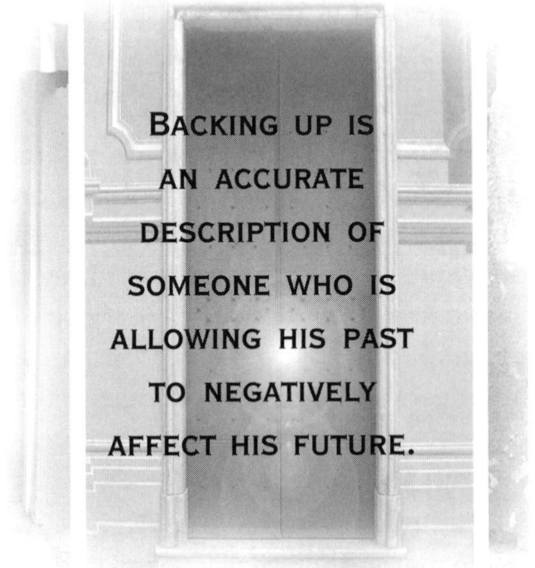

Who shall separate us from the love of Christ? Shall tribulation, or distress, or persecution, or famine, or nakedness, or peril, or sword?

As it is written: "For Your sake we are killed all day long; We are accounted as sheep for the slaughter."

Yet in all these things we are more than conquerors through Him who loved us.

For I am persuaded that neither death nor life, nor angels nor principalities nor powers, nor things present nor things to come,

> **nor height nor depth, nor any other created thing, shall be able to separate us from the love of God which is in Christ Jesus our Lord (Romans 8:35-39).**

One thing noticeably absent from Paul's list is the past. The past does not hinder God from loving us but it can separate us from experiencing His love if we allow it to. Paul revealed his own method for overcoming the past:

> **Not that I have already attained, or am already perfected; but I press on, that I may lay hold of that for which Christ Jesus has also laid hold of me.**
>
> **Brethren, I do not count myself to have apprehended; but one thing I do, forgetting those things which are behind and reaching forward to those things which are ahead,**
>
> **I press toward the goal for the prize of the upward call of God in Christ Jesus" (Philippians 3:12-14).**

It is impossible to forget something by trying to do so. The very act of identifying things we should forget fortifies them in our memory. How do you shut the door on those things which are behind? Paul summed it up in three short words, "I press toward." The word **"press"** means pursue and is translated as *persecuted* over twenty-five times in the New Testament. Paul focused on his destiny and pursued it with all the energy and zeal that he once used when he persecuted the church. His energetic **"reaching forward"** to other things and determining to obtain God's highest for his life enabled him to overcome his past. He shut the door on the things behind him by continuing to forcefully knock on the doors before him. We must not let the past imprison our potential for future fruitfulness in God. Just as Elisha exhorted the impoverished widow, we must shut the door behind us.

Asking for Help

God's solution to the widow's adversity involved asking others for help. Though she had the little jar of oil, without her neighbor's empty vessels her miracle would have never happened. God has ordered life in such a way that we need one another. Paul's revelation of the church as being the body of Christ concludes that to function well we must function in harmony with each member playing its proper roll.

Many of us are unwilling to ask anyone for help, but doing so is essential for us to succeed. Pride is one of God's greatest enemies, and He requires us to humble ourselves to share in the grace of His enabling power.

Determining the Measure

Amazing as it may seem, neither Elisha the prophet nor the Lord determined the size of the miracle. The widow herself determined it by how many vessels she secured to pour oil into. Preparation often determines the success of any venture. In the early years of NASA space travel, a man once went to Cape Canaveral where the U.S. government was building launch pads for the first trips to the moon. The man looked way down into the deep hole being built for the pad and called down to the tiny man in the bottom of the hole, "What are you doing down there?" The man looked up, scratched his head and said, "We are going to the moon!"

The release of heaven's abundance is often determined by our response here on earth. He wants to do much more for us and through us than we can imagine. Many say that they are waiting on God to do the supernatural while the truth is that we are at fault and not Him:

> **Yes, again and again they tempted God, and limited the Holy One of Israel.**
>
> **They did not remember His power: The day when He redeemed them from the enemy,**
>
> **When He worked His signs in Egypt, and His wonders in the field of Zoan (Psalm 78:41-43).**

We have limited the Lord by our own unbelief and disobedience.

Jesus taught that we often determine the measure of our blessings. He said that men would give to us in the same way that we also give:

> **"Give, and it will be given to you: good measure, pressed down, shaken together, and running over will be put into your bosom. For with the same measure that you use, it will be measured back to you" (Luke 6:38).**

Paul also taught this truth:

> **But this I say: He who sows sparingly will also reap sparingly, and he who sows bountifully will also reap bountifully.**
>
> **So let each one give as he purposes in his heart, not grudgingly or of necessity; for God loves a cheerful giver.**
>
> **And God is able to make all grace abound toward you, that you, always having all sufficiency in all things, may have an abundance for every good work (II Corinthians 9:6-8).**

All of us need the supernatural resources of heaven released on our behalf. One of the keys to living in the supernatural realm lies in this aspect of living by faith. If we will give, He will be sure we are given to. If we will faithfully prepare for His miraculous power we will not be disappointed by what transpires. The widow woke up one day in debt, in fear of losing her sons to slavery, with but an insignificant jar of oil. By sundown she went to bed as a regional distributor.

Nothing but a Jar of Oil

The widow had God's provision in her midst and did not know it. Jacob discovered this truth while fleeing for his life from his estranged brother Esau. As he camped at Luz he dreamed of a ladder set up on the earth that reached into heaven itself. The angels of God were going up and down on the ladder. They speak of the angels who minister heaven's resources to the heirs of salvation upon the earth.

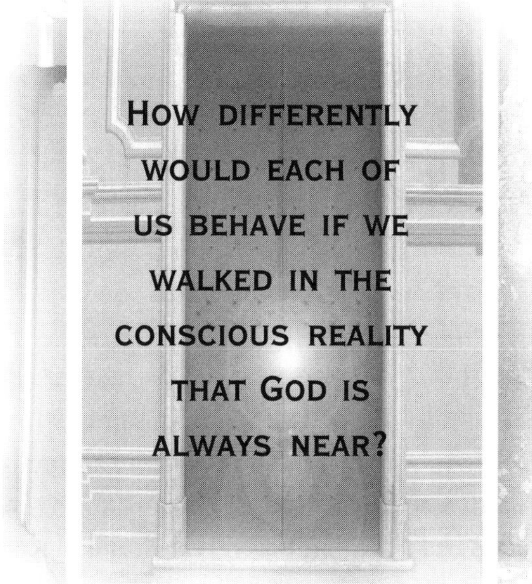

The Lord Himself stood at the top and promised to protect and provide for Jacob and his descendants. Greatly surprised and amazed Jacob exclaimed to himself, **"Surely the Lord is in this place, and I did not know it" (Genesis 28:16).** God is always near, but so often we do not recognize Him. The Lord revealed Himself to Jacob and assured him that He was with him and that He always had been.

> **"Behold, I am with you and will keep you wherever you go, and will bring you back to this land; for I will not leave you until I have done what I have spoken to you" (verse 15).**

The Lord was with Jacob in Luz and He was with him while he was swindling his brother, Esau out of the elder brother's blessing. God wanted Jacob to know He was always there. How differently would each of us behave if we walked in the conscious reality that God is always near? Our challenge is to recognize Him and conform to His wishes. In the life of the widow woman, He was present with her and provided for her in her darkest hour. He was in the small jar of oil, waiting to be released.

The Oil

The insignificant jar of oil used to prosper the widow and her family is also a biblical type of the anointing of the Holy Spirit, the empowerment God provides each believer. We are tempted to disregard this most valuable possession because it seems so elusive and small. Sometimes we feel anointed and function well in our ministry, but at other times we feel nothing at all and yet we must still function. I have been amazed at how often the Lord does some of the most impressive things when the feeling of the anointing is hardly discernible. Just like the widow, our job is not primarily to feel but to obey and pour. We must take the little that we have and use it, while leaving the results to Him. We must be faithful to function in our calling with the resources at hand.

What We Disregard God Often Uses

"Nothing but a jar of oil!" The widow's pathetic response to the prophet's question contains a clue to what motivates the Lord. He often uses what we disregard because He wants to be known for who He is and what He can do. It is one of His fundamental characteristics. Paul acknowledges this truth about the Lord:

But God has chosen the foolish things of the world to put to shame the wise, and God has chosen the weak things of the world to put to shame the things which are mighty;

and the base things of the world and the things which are despised God has chosen, and the things which are not, to bring to nothing the things that are,

that no flesh should glory in His presence (I Corinthians 1:27-29).

The foolish things, the weak things, the base things, the despised things, even things that do not exist, are the very things God chooses to glorify Himself. We must understand this vital truth. Many times we look at the pitiful things we have on hand, then we look at the mountain of human dilemma with dismay. We shake our heads and walk away from the plan of God convinced by our own unbelief that all is lost. However, God likes those situations because He has hidden His vast wealth and power in those very places. He used the humiliation and utter weakness of Christ Jesus' death on the cross to defeat Satan. It was always His plan, even from the very beginning. If God's principle of using weakness to destroy demonic strength was important enough to be included in His original strategy, then it should be important to us now. God will use what men often disregard. We must learn to identify our resources.

Unlocking Our Potential

The acorn contains the forest; it just does not look like it. The jar of oil contained the solution to the impending poverty and slavery the widow woman faced. She just did not see it at first. God hides His power and ability in small places and puts them in every life. Our challenge is to recognize them in our own lives and handle them in such a way that His potential can be unlocked. ■

What Does God Require?

by Mike Roberts

Anyone who has a job knows what it means to be accountable. Those in authority within a company or business have certain requirements and expectations of the employees. Because of this, it is important for the employees to understand what is expected and required of them.

The same is true in our walk with God. The Bible says that we will all one day stand before the judgment seat of the Lord (see II Corinthians 5:10). At some point, all of us will be held accountable to God for the deeds that we have done during our lives on earth. Therefore, it is very important we understand what God requires of us.

What Do You Think?

So, what does God require? Chances are, if you asked a hundred people that question, you would hear nearly one hundred different answers. Some would probably say that God requires us to attend church and read the Bible. Others might say that we should spend a certain length of time in prayer each day. Most would probably agree that God requires us to stop being bad and start being good. For example, we should never lie, cheat, or steal, and we should give money to the church.

Obviously, all of the things listed above are good things to do. However, in our attempts to juggle all the different "do's" and "don'ts," it is easy to perceive God's requirements as being more complicated than they truly are. Many people live with a secret fear and guilt that they are not living up to God's standards, even though they are sincere in their faith and are trying to please the Lord with their lives.

The Old Testament prophet Micah asked the very question "what does God require," and the answer he provided is surprisingly simple. Here is what he said:

> **With what shall I come to the Lord and bow myself before the God on high? Shall I come to Him with burnt offerings, with yearling calves?**
>
> **Does the Lord take delight in thousands of rams, in ten thousand rivers of oil? Shall I present my first-born for my rebellious acts, the fruit of my body for the sin of my soul?**
>
> **He has told you, O man, what is good; and what does the Lord require of you but to do justice, to love kindness, and to walk humbly with your God? (Micah 6:6-8)**

IT IS IMPORTANT TO UNDERSTAND THAT THERE ARE CERTAIN THINGS GOD FORBIDS—NOT BECAUSE HE IS BORING AND RIGID, BUT BECAUSE HE WANTS THE BEST FOR US.

Micah first listed several things that portray what many people commonly believe: God requires offerings and sacrifices. Many of us have the tendency to focus on what we have to do to meet God's expectations and gain His approval. However, as Micah explained, all God truly requires can be summed up in three things: **"to do justice, to love kindness,"** or some versions of Scripture read **"to love mercy,"** and to **"walk humbly"** with Him. Many times we are concerned with what we have to do, but God is far more concerned with who we are. We tend to feel like we have to work to *attain* God's righteousness, but once we accept the Lord, we *become* His righteousness. II Corinthians 5:21 says:

> **He made Him who knew no sin to be sin on our behalf, so that we might become the righteousness of God in Him.**

God does not require that we live in accordance with a list of rules. Instead He desires that we live with Him in an intimate, personal relationship. This relationship is available to us because of what He has done, not because of what we do. Once we have been saved, what we do is done on the basis of having His acceptance, not to receive it.

It is important to understand that there are certain things God forbids—not because He is boring and rigid, but because He wants the best for us. As Benjamin Franklin explained, *"Sin is not hurtful because it is forbidden, but it is forbidden because it is hurtful."* God forbids certain things because they are harmful to us and to our relationship with Him. He wants us to be free from the entanglements of sin so that we are able to walk with Him the way He desires.

As we live our lives with the Lord, and walk with Him in an intimate relationship, we will be empowered to do what He requires from us—justice, kindness, and mercy, and a humble walk with Him.

Let us take a closer look at these three requirements.

To Do Justice

"To do justice" is the first thing Micah said God requires of us. In Psalm 89:14, David says to the Lord:

> **Righteousness and justice are the foundation of Your throne...(NKJV).**

Our God, who is the King of kings, sits on a throne that is founded upon righteousness and justice. Justice is fundamentally a part of the Lord's character, as Isaiah understood:

> **For the Lord is a God of justice...(Isaiah 30:18).**
>
> **For I, the Lord, love justice... (Isaiah 61:8).**

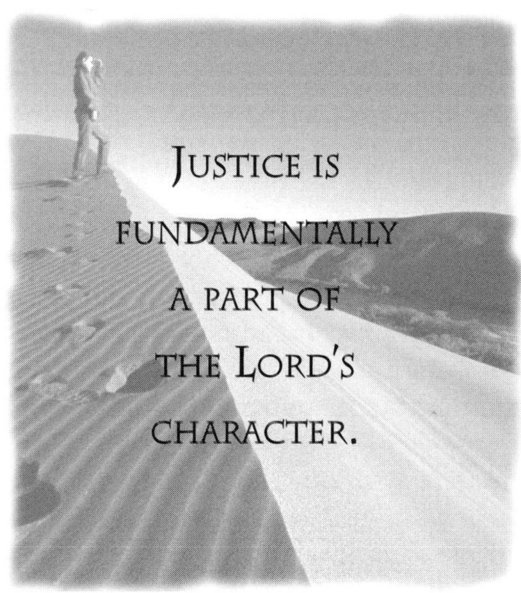

To do justice basically means to be impartial in our dealings with other people and to treat them the way we want to be treated. Proverbs 11:1 says:

> **A false balance is an abomination to the Lord, but a just weight is His delight.**

Deuteronomy 25:14-16 says:

> **You shall not have in your house differing measures, a large and a small.**
>
> **You shall have a full and a just weight; you shall have a full and just measure, that your days may be prolonged in the land which the Lord your God gives you.**
>
> **For everyone who does these things, everyone who acts unjustly is an abomination to the Lord your God.**

These verses imply a proactive approach on our part to be Christ-like in the way we treat other people. Jesus Himself said:

> **In everything therefore, treat people the same way you want them to treat you, so treat them, for this is the Law and the Prophets (Matthew 7:12).**

This verse has become known as the "Golden Rule," and Jesus said it sums up all that the Law entails. We must not discriminate based on gender, race, or age, and we must not withhold from someone what rightly belongs to them. This applies to every area of our lives, whether personal, professional, in the church, or in the marketplace.

To Love Kindness and Mercy

Just as doing justice has to do with how we treat other people, loving-kindness and mercy has to do with how we respond to the way other people treat us. Jesus said:

> **And if you love those who love you, what credit is that to you? For even sinners love those who love them.**

And if you do good to those who do good to you, what credit is that to you? For even sinners do the same.

And if you lend to those from whom you expect to receive, what credit is that to you? Even sinners lend to sinners, in order to receive back the same amount.

But love your enemies, and do good, and lend, expecting nothing in return; and your reward will be great, and you will be sons of the Most High; for He Himself is kind to ungrateful and evil men.

Be merciful, just as your Father is merciful (Luke 6:32-36).

WE MUST CHOOSE TO GUARD OUR HEARTS AGAINST BITTERNESS AND ANGER, AND RESPOND MERCIFULLY TO THE PERSON OR PERSONS WHO OFFEND US.

Kindness and mercy are inseparable characteristics of the nature of God, and He demonstrates them justly to all men, even **"to ungrateful and evil men."** The Bible says that He is patient and does not want anyone to perish, but for every person to come to repentance (see II Peter 3:9). It is actually God's kindness, not His anger or judgment that leads us to repentance (see Romans 2:4). Just as God is merciful and kind with us, we must be merciful and kind as we respond to others. If we simply treat them the way they treat us, we are only doing what sinners would do. The Lord has a higher standard for us as we deal with others. He wants us to truly love one another, and true love will produce justice, kindness, and mercy.

Dealing With Offenses

Jesus assured us that in this life we would have to deal with offenses (see Luke 17:1). We cannot always prevent offenses, but when they come, we must respond to them appropriately. God has never wronged anyone, yet He shows mercy when we wrong Him. We must do the same. Offenses may come even when we are completely innocent, but we must choose to show mercy when someone wrongs us.

Additionally, we must be careful to guard our hearts. If we choose to take the offense personally, it can cause us a great deal of trouble. It can negatively impact our relationships, distort our vision, consume our thoughts and emotions, and even affect our health. Above all, it will interfere with our relationship with the Lord. We must choose to guard our hearts against bitterness and anger, and respond mercifully to the person or persons who offend us. We cannot control what others do, but our response will determine the full effect the offense has in our lives. With an attitude of humility, we must return good for evil. I Peter 3:8-9 says:

...let all be harmonious, sympathetic, brotherly, kind-hearted, and humble in spirit;

not returning evil for evil, or insult for insult, but giving a blessing instead; for you were called for this very purpose that you might inherit a blessing.

Here Peter exhorted us to be "**humble in spirit**" in all that we do. This brings us to the third thing the Lord requires of us—humility. There is no other way to walk with God except in a spirit of humility. I Peter 5:5-7 says:

...God is opposed to the proud, but gives grace to the humble.

Humble yourselves, therefore, under the mighty hand of God, that He may exalt you at the proper time,

casting all your anxiety upon Him, because He cares for you.

To whatever degree we are walking in pride, to that same degree our relationship with the Lord will be hindered. All sin will interfere with our relationship with the Lord, but pride is one sin that will actually bring us an encounter with God's opposition. As Rick Joyner has often explained, it would be better to have every demon in hell chasing us than to have God opposing us. However, when we have a spirit of humility, we qualify ourselves for God's grace, which will enable us to walk with Him and be the kind of people He has called us to be.

Pride and Humility

Humility may be one of the most misunderstood of the Christian virtues. Obviously, humility is the opposite of pride, but many times what we think of as humility may actually be pride. Likewise, many things that we might think of as pride may actually be humility. Pride is when we feel like we are or have to be sufficient in ourselves apart from God. C.S. Lewis once said, *"A man is never so proud as when striking an attitude of humility."* Humility is when we choose to trust in the strength and power of the Lord, and not in our own abilities or lack of abilities.

Apart from God we have nothing, but in God we have everything. Pride is essentially self-centered, while humility is essentially God-centered. When the apostle Paul said that he could do all things through Christ who gives him the strength (see Philippians 4:13), imagine how proud that could have sounded. Such a statement could be rooted in pride, but Paul's confidence was in the Lord, not in his own ability. When the Lord called Moses to lead His people out of Egypt, Moses offered a list of reasons why he could not do it: "Who am I that I should go? They're not going to listen to me. I can't even speak very well!" To the natural mind, Moses might have seemed humble, but he was actually quite proud. He thought he knew better than the Lord did. His trust was in his inability, and he was walking in self-centered pride (see Exodus chapters 3 and 4).

THE MOST IMPORTANT THING WE NEED TO UNDERSTAND IS THAT GOD LOVES US, AND HIS GREATEST DESIRE IS A PERSONAL, INTIMATE RELATIONSHIP WITH US.

Subtle Forms of Pride

Humility is when our trust and confidence are in the Lord. The goal of the enemy is to interfere in our walk with the Lord, so he has a list of subtle schemes to cause our trust and confidence to be in ourselves. Anxiety, stress, worry, fear, guilt, and condemnation are all very subtle forms of pride. They cause us to strive to solve our problems with our own strength and abilities, but we are unable to receive a full measure of God's grace in our situations as long as are walking in pride.

For example, let us consider why Peter exhorted us to cast all of our anxiety upon the Lord at the same time he was telling us to humble ourselves. That almost appears to be two separate thoughts, but Peter understood that anxiety is actually pride. It causes us to trust in our own ability and our own wisdom, and not the Lord. Paul said:

> **Be anxious for nothing, but in everything by prayer and supplication with thanksgiving let your requests be known to God.**
>
> **And the peace of God, which surpasses all comprehension, shall guard your hearts and your minds in Christ Jesus (Philippians 4:6-7).**

While the enemy wants to make us anxious, the Lord wants to give us a peace that will guard our hearts and minds. It is only from this place of humility that we are truly effective in dealing with problems anyway, for our trust is in the Lord and His grace.

The most important thing we need to understand is that God loves us, and His greatest desire is a personal, intimate relationship with us. If we truly seek Him, we will find Him. As we walk with Him in a spirit of humility, we will walk continually in His grace and peace. This will enable us to be confident and victorious in every aspect of our lives and in our relationships with other people. Let us press on to know the Lord and be like Him. In doing so we will experience abundant life with Him and each other.

> **But if we walk in the light as He Himself is in the light, we have fellowship with one another, and the blood of Jesus His Son cleanses us from all sin (I John 1:7).** ■

C.S. Lewis, "Christianity and Culture" from *The Collected Works of C.S. Lewis,* p. 182, Inspirational Press Edition, 1996.

Buried Treasure

All Scriptures are New International Version.

by Andrew P. Surace

> **When I saw in the plunder a beautiful robe from Babylonia, two hundred shekels of silver and a wedge of gold weighing fifty shekels, I coveted them and took them. They are hidden in the ground inside my tent, with the silver underneath (Joshua 7:21).**

Some treasures we bury—some end up burying us. This is the story of Achan. Achan was a soldier on the winning side, a husband, a father, and unfortunately, a thief. It was the last title that buried him. Joshua had clearly stated that certain spoils of the victory at Jericho were to be set apart for the Lord. It was made very clear that anyone touching these devoted things would bring destruction to their lives. Isn't it always the forbidden fruit that causes the greatest temptation? Like Judas, Achan had a problem with things—they owned him instead of him having ownership over them. We have two main lessons we can learn from this.

First, we see that a lust for things is every bit as dangerous as sexual lust for a man or a woman. The church talks much about sexual sin and lust, but the Bible says that it is the **"love of money" (I Timothy 6:10)** that is the root of all evil. Isn't it funny that in a capitalistic society such as ours, sins that involve money do not get much press? Yet, we may make the argument from this passage that it can be even a little more deadly.

Now here is an interesting question: What do Judas, Ananias, Saphira, and

Achan all have in common? They all had a problem with materialism until they all lost their lives and the possessions they thought were so important. By comparison, God was much more gracious to Rahab, the harlot, and the prostitute woman at the well.

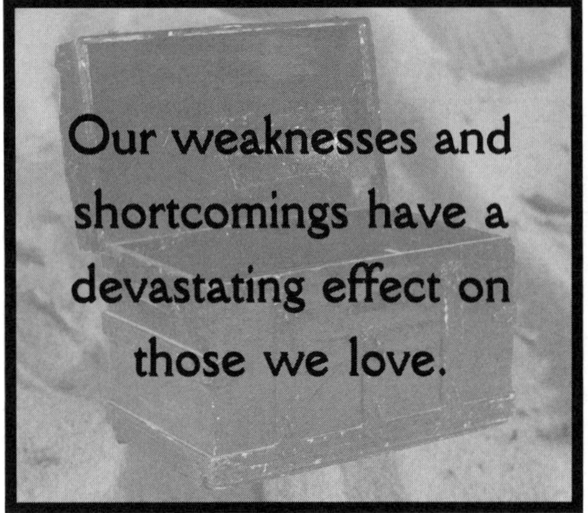

I am not trying to make a theology out of this; I am only trying to show that greed and coveting that which is not ours are dangerous sins. In addition, if these sins are not dealt with and repented of, they can lead to death. To put it simply, coveting is a desire for those things that God has not given you. Perhaps God has even clearly told you that you cannot have them.

In Achan's case, the desire turned to the actual taking of those things. Although sexual sins get much more attention in the church today, God does not overlook these sometimes more socially acceptable sins. It may even come as a surprise to some that two of the Ten Commandments have to do with possessions while only one has to do with sex (see Exodus 20). From this little fact, one could make the argument that it is twice as easy to sin when it comes to materialism as it is to sin sexually.

One of the great benefits of the tithe is to keep this deadly desire to idolize possessions under control. As we regularly give ten percent of our money to the Lord (for those who may not know, that is what it means to tithe), we are helping to break the back of greed and covetousness in our lives. Also, keep in mind that God clearly states the tithe is holy and belongs to Him. Therefore, to hold on to what is His is stealing and worse yet, stealing from God (see Malachi 3:8-12).

The point here is that whether it is sexual sin, greed, or pride, no one sins alone. Although Achan seemed to have sinned alone (we have no real record that his family took part in his sin), they paid the price along with him. Because of his unrestrained lust for things, his whole family paid the ultimate price. The sins of our lives are carried into the lives of those we love. Our weaknesses and shortcomings have a devastating effect on those we love. The alcoholic who never seems to make it home with his check brings great pain and shame to his family. *He may drink alone, but he does not sin alone.*

What are you bringing into your house and what effect might it have on your children and loved ones? I am sure Achan never intended to involve his family with his sin, but as we see they helped pay the price. All of Achan's family were destroyed because of disobedience and an uncontrolled desire for things. Sin is infectious! If you will keep it out of your heart, it can never get into your house. ■

This devotion is an excerpt from Andrew P. Surace's new book, ***Stepping Stones Along the Path of Life.*** It is available through our catalog and website or by ordering through our toll free number at **1-800-542-0278.**

WE WILL NOT BE SHAKEN

All Scriptures are New International Version unless otherwise indicated.

by Amanda Coalson

A Bible teacher I once knew said, "If you're feeling a little dry, sink your roots deeper into the earth, for it is in the deep that you will find the water that satisfies." I can still hear her words in my mind and I am still inspired by them. She not only encouraged me to sink deeper in my pursuit of the Lord, but her words also inspired me to study trees and their growth, especially their roots.

I knew the roots of a tree were vital for the life of a tree. However, I never thought much about roots until the Lord impressed it upon my heart, and revealed the different functions of roots and the ways we can apply these things to our spiritual lives. The function of the root is to absorb water and minerals from the soil, to transport these to the rest of the tree, to serve as a reservoir for food, and to anchor the tree to the ground. Thus, roots are the "underground tree."

Roots grow in a similar way to branches, but they grow downward, while branches grow upward and out. The root produces lateral branches, and then branches out again in length, slowly producing a whole fibrous system. The part of the root that grows is called the root tip, and it is only an inch long and as thin as thread. We have all tried to pull a weed out of the ground, only to hear ripping and end up with just a small portion of the roots still attached to the original plant. This is because the roots are anchored to the soil by microscopically fine root hairs. These root hairs are short-lived, continually being replaced, and literally numbering in the billions.

I Corinthians 3:7 says, "**So neither he who plants nor he who waters is anything, but only God, who makes things grow.**" God is the One who makes everything grow. He who makes the roots of every plant grow into the earth also makes our roots grow deep into Him. Philippians 2:13 says, "**for it is God who works in you both to will and to act according to his good purpose.**" This should give us peace. The trees do not have to strain to grow—they just grow and grow. We do not have to strain to grow in the Lord. We will come across storms, but the Lord will keep us strong, firm, and steadfast if we trust in Him. We will not be shaken when we sink our roots in Him through trust.

Studies show some amazing facts about the roots of the rye plant. After only four months of growth, this plant develops an average total of 378 miles of roots! The average speed of root growth was found to be three miles per day. The total surface of the root hairs alone was found to exceed the entire floor surface area of three or four houses. All of this was contained within a volume of soil that measured only about two cubic feet! This is why that plant is so hard to pull up.

The density of the root hairs—the 6,500 square feet packed into two cubic feet makes me think of the richness of the Lord inside of us. We all have a vast network of roots inside of us, waiting to go deeper and wider in the Lord. Our root hairs are our individual experiences with the Lord. These experiences are made daily, weekly, monthly, and are often built upon. They symbolize the times the Lord has spoken to us in a special way, or the time we laid something down in sacrifice before the Lord. Our roots are the deep times with the Lord, the times we will never forget.

We must never measure our whole root system by one root hair, meaning that we must never measure our spiritual growth by one experience or one day. What we daily experience and what we see is but a thread of root. It is woven in, but it is not the whole. In the ground, billions of root hairs may seem tangled, but they are all working together to gather nutrients. I do not think all the individual hairs "know" about all the other hairs; they are just doing their job. So we do not see how everything fits together. We must always remember that we cannot see the whole picture. We just gather nutrients for the time being.

A Reservoir in Dry Times

Roots also serve as a reservoir for food during dry times. The memories of our awesome times with the Lord are those reservoirs. I remember a time, almost a year ago, when I was pretty dry spiritually. I knew the Lord wanted me to move to Charlotte to attend the MorningStar School of Ministry, but I had little money to get there. I was nervous and anxious about how I was going to get to school, where I was going to live, and how I was going to survive once I got there. I remember really crying out to the Lord one night in particular while I was worshiping. I was broken, crying, and incredibly scared. However, the Lord was with me and I knew He had called me to MorningStar. So I decided to praise God. The very next day someone gave me a substantial check. This check helped me get to Charlotte, and my life would have been much harder without it.

Paul says in Ephesians, **"...that you, being rooted and grounded in love, may be able to comprehend with all the saints what is the width and length and depth and height—to know the love of Christ which passes knowledge; that you may be filled with all the fullness of God" (Ephesians 3:17-19 NKJV).** The language used makes me think of trees—the width, length, depth, and height—that we may be rooted and grounded in love. We all start small, like a little germinated seed, but immediately begin growing down. We grow and stretch to find the nutrients and water in our soil. We search for God in the deep places during the dark times, and as we do this, we are becoming rooted and grounded in love. Love is our soil; though it is sometimes dry, our supernatural root system finds what it needs to become deep and wide.

The Importance of Growing Daily

I discovered in my study that roots grow all the time. They grow at night and during the day, when it rains and when it is dry, in the summer, and yes in the winter. We, too, are always growing. We may often wonder if our day-to-day experiences and findings are important. Too many days pass by when nothing seems to happen. However, the Lord assures us that every day is necessary for growth. Every day, every inch, every step is working for an eternal planting, something we will only see in the spring. In spring our leaves are big and showy, our growth and beauty evident to all who pass by. Yet in the winter we may seem to die. We seem to shrink back because of the elements, but we never cease to grow. We must always remember that God causes all things to grow, and not we ourselves. He makes everything beautiful in its time. Yes, spring will come and we will bear much fruit. In the spring, we will look around and again see our big, showy leaves and smile with satisfaction.

...the true nourishment will come when we sink our roots deeper and continue to pursue the Lord.

If you are feeling a little dry, thirsty, and you want more, go deeper—go to the Word. The teacher who inspired this study challenged us to dig deeper into the Word. I am not always in awe when I read the Bible. Some days when I read, I feel like I am getting nothing out of the Word. However, I know the Lord is depositing things inside of me, even if I do not "feel" like He is. He is teaching all of us, especially when we do not understand what He is doing. It is important that we continue to read our Bibles when we are not sure if we are getting anything. When we do not feel like we are getting anything, the true nourishment will come when we sink our roots deeper and continue to pursue the Lord. He is the One who is at work in us; it is not up to us to make ourselves grow.

Roots also serve to anchor the tree to the ground. Mature sequoias are by far the most massive living things on earth. The weight of the trunk of the General Sherman Sequoia, found in California's Sequoia National Park, is 625 tons. The total weight of this tree is estimated at more than 1,000 tons. It stretches at least 272 feet in the sky and still is not the tallest of its kind!

As huge as sequoias are, their roots are relatively shallow, rarely going deeper than ten feet. How do these trees stand? Their roots can occupy an area larger than an acre because they grow out and not just down. The redwood trees also have this shallow root system, but are often found in groups. The roots of trees in a forest may be more shallow than a tree standing alone, but nevertheless secure because their roots are intertwined under the ground. Their intertwining provides a strong structure that will support the forest when mighty winds blow.

We, too, must grow out and not just down. When we connect with other believers, we will be stronger. If one redwood stood alone, it would have a much greater chance of falling. If we do not stay connected with other believers, we will surely fall.

Stand Strong

When I was very young, a tornado came through our neighborhood, destroying homes, roads, and of course, plant life. I remember walking through our demolished backyard looking at the roots of the trees the wind had knocked down. I was not amazed at the time because I was six, but now I am amazed. I remember the trees that were knocked down were at the edge of the forest. The trees in the middle of the forest were intact. From this, I see that we all need to surround ourselves with other believers who are grounded in truth. When we stand alone, we will not have very much to hang on to. But when we join together with others in deep places, we will stand strong when the winds blow. Like the mighty redwoods, we must all stand together and intertwine our roots to form one vast, strong structure.

I have said everything to say this: We will not be shaken when we trust the Lord. When we nurture our experiences with the Lord, when we continue though things that are hard, and when we connect with other believers, we are sinking our roots deeper. If we do these things, we will not be shaken. We must always remember that the Lord is establishing us; it is not up to us to grow ourselves. Any tree, no matter how large or amazing, depends on the Lord to grow. Jeremiah 17:7-8 says, **"But blessed is the man who trusts in the Lord, whose confidence is in him. He will be like a tree planted by the water that sends out its roots by the stream. It does not fear when heat comes; its leaves are always green. It has no worries in a year of drought and never fails to bear fruit."** If you are feeling a little dry, sink your roots deeper. ■

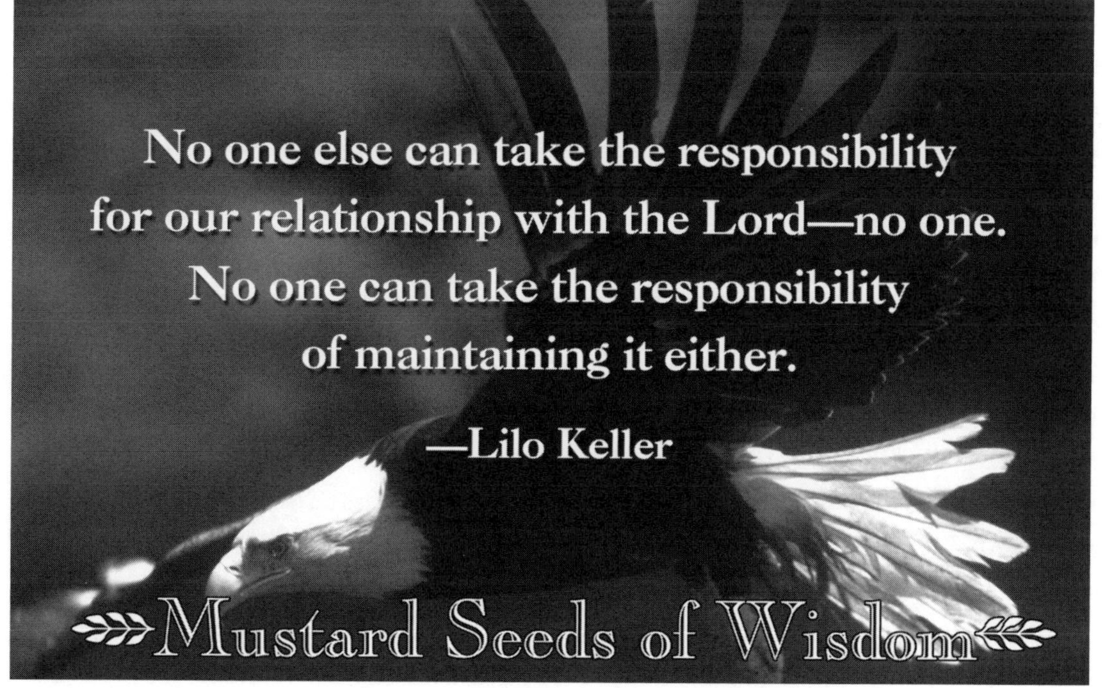

Seven Presuppositional & Foundational *Principles of the* Kingdom of God

by Bob Mumford

My search for understanding the kingdom dates back to 1963 when I taught a Bible class at Elim Bible Institute. One day the Lord told me to put my lessons aside and open the kingdom of God to the students. I did not even know what I was going to say, but once we focused on the kingdom, the Holy Spirit fell on that classroom. The class was supposed to dismiss at 10 a.m., but we did not leave until 3 o'clock that afternoon. During those hours, the seed concepts of the kingdom were born in my own understanding and they have been growing ever since.

There are very few biblical definitions of the kingdom of God. The nearest to a definition would be Romans 14:17, **"for the kingdom of God is not eating and drinking, but righteousness and peace and joy in the Holy Spirit."** Due to its enormity and spiritual nature, the kingdom is ineffable. It is the thrust of the whole New Testament. The following are seven foundational presuppositions that have helped me better understand the kingdom of God:

1. *God's Nature or DNA.* The kingdom of God expresses the character or nature of the Father as the source of His government, rule, or realm. It follows, then, that all conceptual understanding of the kingdom must include an expression of God's DNA—that is, His own nature as self-revealed in the seven hidden attributes of God's Person: compassion,

graciousness, slow to anger, mercy, truth, covenantally faithful, and forgiving (see Exodus 34:6-7).

2. *Father's Rule.* God's kingdom (government, rule, or realm) became incarnate in the Person of His Son, our Lord Jesus Christ. God is Spirit (see John 4:24), God is Light (see I John 1:5), and God is Agape (see I John 4:8). The absence of the Greek article "a" in these three statements speaks of Who God is, not a quality that He possesses. The incarnation of Agape causes us to know that this Spirit-Being is personal and that His Light is life-giving. God, as a Father, gave the kingdom to His Son, Who was able to say, **"He who has seen Me has seen the Father" (John 14:9).** The Father and the Son committed the kingdom to the Person of the Holy Spirit for the bringing forth of the fruit of the kingdom—love, joy, peace, good temper, kindness, generosity, fidelity, gentleness, and self-control (see Galatians 5:22-23). It is this fruit of the Spirit that produces sons and daughters of the kingdom (see Matthew 13:38; Hebrew 2:10). It is on the biblical premise that God is Light and Life that we can say, **"for the kingdom of God is... in the Holy Spirit" (Romans 14:17).**

3. *Transformation.* The kingdom can be seen and entered into only by being born from above and by means of water and Spirit baptism. In our new birth, the eternal Seed is implanted within us (see I Peter 1:23). This eternal Seed can be neglected or nourished. As the Seed is nourished, all that is self-referential and fearful in us is exposed and our primal distrust in God as a Father is displaced by His *Agape* (see Romans 5:5-8). It is the eternal Seed, *Agape* Incarnate, which overcomes the world. As we embrace *Agape*, which is the glory and DNA of the Father, we are transformed (see II Corinthians 3:18) and consequently, we extend His governmental influence for society's transformation.

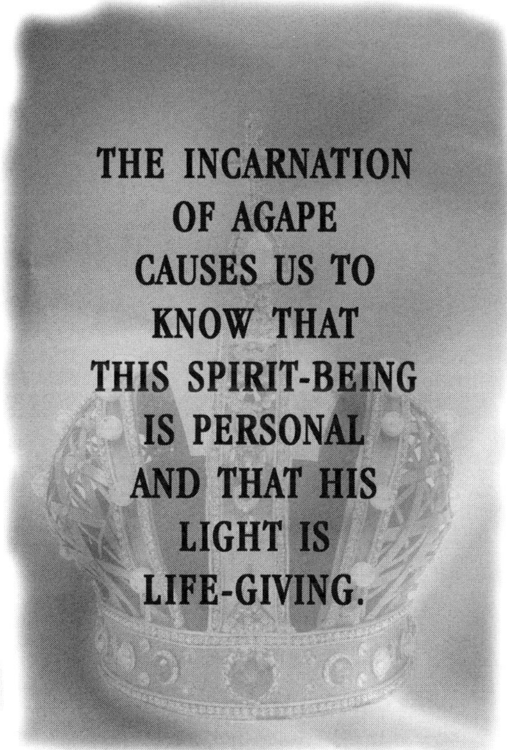

4. *Relational Cultivation.* While misdirected emphases on subordinate issues such as prosperity, distorted evangelism, mega-church, and dubious displays of the supernatural, etc., are often successful, the primary issue of the kingdom is the relational cultivation of the sons and daughters of the kingdom

(see II Corinthians 6:17-18; Matthew 13:38). Producing sons and daughters of glory means we have regained the capacity to transform our being from dream-stealers into dream-enablers (see John 10:10). Historically, it is the kingdom that corrects and adjusts the church. The church does not have the authority nor the capacity to correct or adjust the kingdom, which is God's absolute.

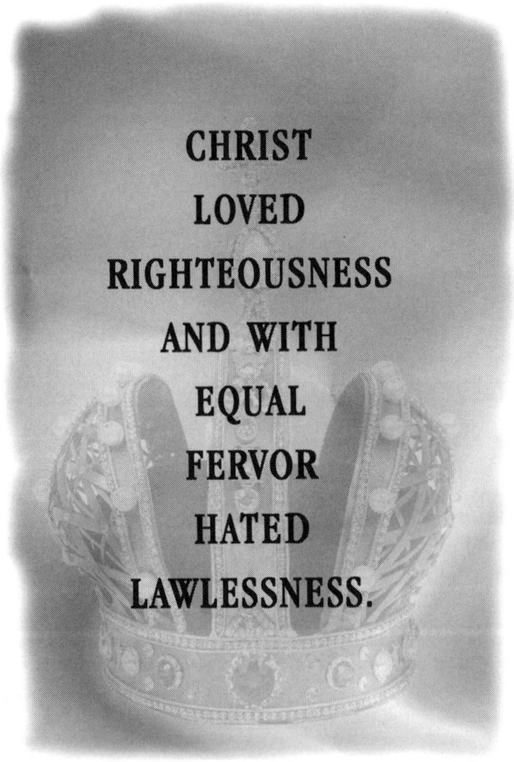

5. *Absolute Truth.* The kingdom of God is the one absolute truth in the universe. From this absolute, all people, philosophy, ethics, and morals are measured (see Acts 17:31). The kingdom creates its own standards and establishes its own rules; it is accountable to none but God, Himself (see Romans 13:8-10). This absolute which governs God's own people is practically and effectively destined to be restored to the entire universe (see Romans 8:19-21; I Corinthians 15:24-28). It is our understanding of this kingdom absolute that enables us to ascertain the practical difference between being culturally captive and controlled versus being culturally sensitive and considerate (see I Corinthians 9:21-23; II Corinthians 5:14).

6. *Systems Cannot Love.* Only people can love. All systems, such as the caste systems in India, the tribal systems in Africa, even the school or prison systems cannot and do not love. Systems take on a life of their own. Most of us have learned not to tangle with cultural systems which have become established tradition. When a local church or a denomination itself becomes a system that takes on a life of its own, it ceases to love in the kingdom sense, developing the capacity to out-live and out-maneuver anyone who would dare challenge its existence. It was the established system of Jesus' day that crucified Him (see Matthew 27:18). The kingdom of God expects Agape to be primary (see Matthew 5:43-48), not systems. We are called to expose, resist, and transform the existing systems that are not in conformity to the absolute principles of God's kingdom (see Ephesians 3:10). Christ loved righteousness and with equal fervor hated lawlessness. This lawlessness would include all personal, corporate/economic, religious, and political systems. Systems are the means by which the

invisible world of spiritual wickedness is able to enter the visible world of human activity (see Ephesians 6:12).

7. *Rest Is a Weapon*. Outside of, or failure to abide in the rest (see Acts 2:25-28; Hebrews 4:11) provided in Christ's perfect redemption, there arises an overwhelming psychology of defeat (see John 14:29-31). God's kingdom is the only known goal in all of life that is worthy of the total loyalty which is expected (see Matthew 13:44-45). Only in the kingdom—not in religion, the church, certainly not in the alternate and competing systems of the world—could it be possible to be promised that to the one who "seeks first the kingdom of God" (see Matthew 6:33), the end result will not shame us in the day of trial or as the Greek would say, "will not turn out wrong" or "will not let you down."

Conclusion

A summary of the kingdom would look like this: Father's Nature, His DNA is Agape. His rule is Agape and the kingdom transformation is to love as He loves. This demands and expects relational primacy; we cannot love God if we do not love our brother. It is the kingdom as relational primacy which is the continual challenge to the church as an institution. Since the kingdom "comes" and cannot be created or domesticated, it demands that we enter His rest by faith, for the expectations of the kingdom are designed to force us into the Person of Christ, who is Agape incarnate. ■

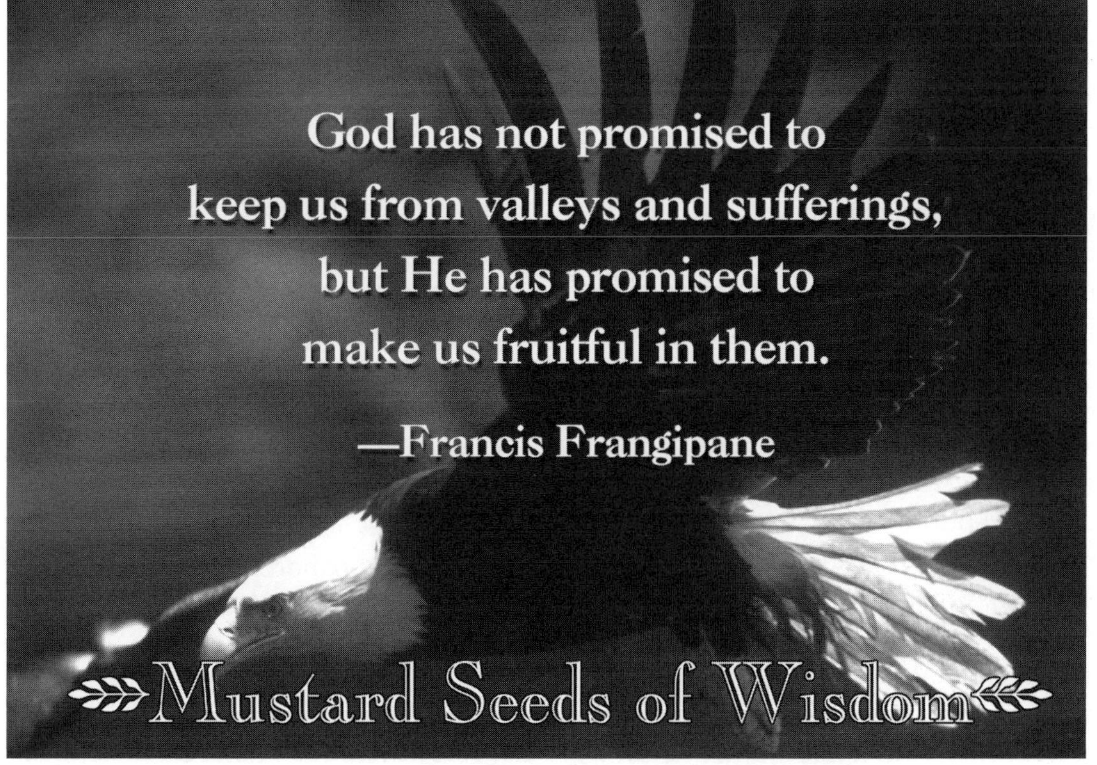

The Cost of Love

by Deborah Joyner Johnson

"Because lawlessness is increased, most people's love will grow cold" (Matthew 24:12).

Lawlessness is increasing throughout society and because of this, **"most people's love will grow cold."** Today fewer people are attending church with pleasure and recreation taking its place. Little "white lies" are told without hesitation. Stealing, cheating, anger, adultery, and sexual promiscuity are happening all around us. Many television shows make such sins seem acceptable by joking about them. Children are watching television more than ever, making deep impressions in them. Some television shows depict parents being dishonored by their children and if that is not bad enough, the parents are also made to look stupid. As a result, young, impressionable minds begin to lose respect, not only for their parents, but for other adults as well. If they are watching any of these type of shows, it is feeding lawlessness to them. This will affect them adversely as they grow into young adults. These are just a few ways lawlessness is creeping into our society.

If we are not staying close to the Lord and His commandments and are exposed to such lawlessness, even Christians can become brainwashed into thinking that such sins are not sins at all. Satan is infiltrating our society in discreet ways, changing the way man believes, making self-gratification more appealing than ever, leading to all kinds of lawlessness.

Cold Love

Self-gratification comes from basically being selfish or self-centered, causing the focus to go inward (personal desires must be met) instead of outward (other's desires must be met). An example of this might be to focus on how something makes a person "feel." A self-gratifying person wants to "feel" good all the time (feeding the flesh), rather than trusting God to provide the desire of his or her heart.

The feeling of love is wonderful, but what happens when feelings become hurt or someone disappoints us? If we are living in self-gratification, then forgiving someone is a very difficult thing to do. It is far easier to be filled with resentment and bitterness, sadly changing this love to a *feeling* of discontentment. The thinking then becomes, "if it doesn't *feel* good, then why bother with it anymore?"

This focus on feelings can become twisted. The fact is if we really love someone it is not about *us*; it is about the other person. We must rise above "feelings" (even disappointments and hurts) for love to stay alive and growing. But how do we accomplish this? We must explore what perfect love is to answer this question.

Jesus, Perfect Love

By studying the life of Jesus, we could *learn* all there is about love, but to truly love others as He did, we must come to *know* Him and be changed into His image, the One Who is the essence of love. His love is perfect. Conditions are not found in His love. He was a Shepherd to the lost, a Friend to sinners, and Healer to the sick simply because He loved them. He taught, nurtured, and loved all people—even the unlovable (the unlovable by our standards—they were never unlovable to Him). He came to give, never expecting anything in return. He was tortured for sins He never committed and suffered the most horrible death imaginable. Even then, in pain inconceivable, He forgave those who were putting Him to death. The very ones who were spitting, laughing, and cursing at Him were the ones He was forgiving. He forgave us for all eternity. This is the perfection of love.

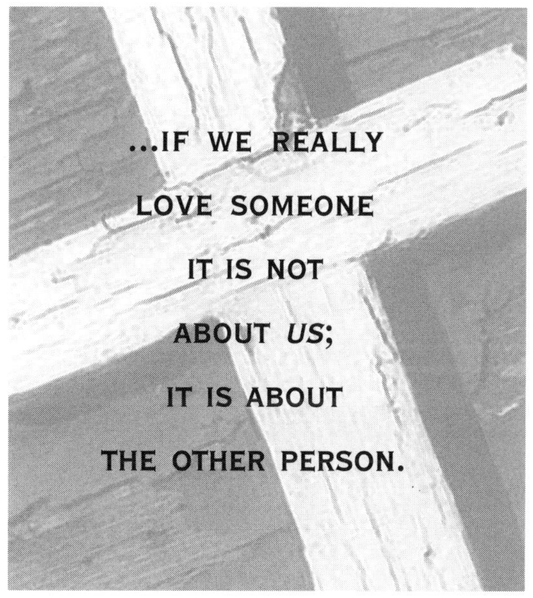

You might say, "Well, that was Jesus and He was perfect. He didn't have to endure what we do in this life. How can we be expected to love as He did?" Jesus went through the same temptations and hardships that we go through in this life and yet He prevailed. We are told in Hebrews 4:15: **"For we do not have a high priest who cannot sympathize with our weaknesses, but One who has been tempted in all things as we are, yet without sin."** He suffered every temptation known to man and still did not sin. He came to earth as a man and had the same feelings that we do, yet He still forgave and loved throughout His life.

To prevent bitterness and resentment from gripping our lives, we must forgive as Jesus did, again and again. How many times should we forgive someone? Jesus gave us the answer.

> **Then Peter came and said to Him, "Lord, how often shall my brother sin against me and I forgive him? Up to seven times?"**
>
> **Jesus said to him, "I do not say to you, up to seven times, but up to seventy times seven" (Matthew 18:21-22).**

WHEN WE GIVE LOVE FREELY, NOT EXPECTING ANYTHING IN RETURN, LOVE WILL GROW NOT ONLY FOR THAT PERSON, BUT HEALING AND RESTORATION WILL BEGIN TO HAPPEN IN BOTH LIVES.

Jesus knows how hard this life is and He even sympathizes with us. He will also help us as Hebrews 4:16 states. **"Therefore let us draw near with confidence to the throne of grace, so that we may receive mercy and find grace to help in time of need."** Jesus will show us how we can love someone if we ask Him to allow us to see the person who offended or hurt us through His eyes. If we ask, He will be faithful to show us why His love is so great for that person. By spending time with the Lord, who is Love, we will become more like Him and take on His characteristics. It is through receiving His love that will enable us to give love to others.

Paul tells us in II Corinthians 5:14: **"for the love of Christ controls us..."** If we do this, then we would be able to love as Jesus does. To love, we must die—die to selfish feelings, anger, resentment, bitterness, and discontentment. We must die when we are hurt, turn the other cheek, forgive, and love with no conditions. Solomon tells us in Proverbs 10:12 that **"Hatred stirs up strife, but love covers all transgressions."** If we love, we can forgive trespasses against us.

By putting that person's needs above our own and working toward fulfilling their needs, love will begin to grow for them. Love has two faces—to receive, but foremost to give. This is where the fulfillment of love will take place. The more we learn to give, the more we will want to give. And in the end we will receive more than we ever thought possible. This will be our reward—our heart will be flooded with love for that person.

When we give love freely, not expecting anything in return, love will grow not only for that person, but healing and restoration will begin to happen in both lives. Love should not be a rarity in our lives, but should be in abundance. The light we have been given is love—His love. By allowing this love to shine forth in our lives, love will begin to grow. Love is the greatest gift we can give on this earth.

What Is Love?

Webster's describes love as a deep and tender affection for or attachment or devotion to a person or persons. The Bible explains love in greater depth.

> **Love is patient, love is kind and is not jealous; love does not brag and is not arrogant,**
>
> **does not act unbecomingly; it does not seek its own, is not provoked, does not take into account a wrong suffered,**
>
> **does not rejoice in unrighteousness, but rejoices with the truth;**
>
> **bears all things, believes all things, hopes all things, endures all things.**
>
> **Love never fails...(I Corinthians 13:4-8).**

Lawlessness will not be an issue in our lives if we will love. Romans 13:8 states: **"Owe nothing to anyone except to love one another; for he who loves his neighbor has fulfilled the law."** We fulfill the law by loving one another, and as a result we will keep God's commandments. We will not commit lawlessness so consequently our love will not grow cold. Paul goes on to say: **Love does no wrong to a neighbor; therefore love is the fulfillment of the law (Romans 13:10).** If we love, we will not break the law, but rather fulfill it.

God loves us as we are. He is simply asking us to love others as He has loved us. He died to save us; we must die to our "selfishness" and love even those we consider unlovable. We can love through Him. Then we will know that His love has been perfected in us.

> **Beloved, if God so loved us, we also ought to love one another...if we love one another, God abides in us, and His love is perfected in us (I John 4:11-12).**

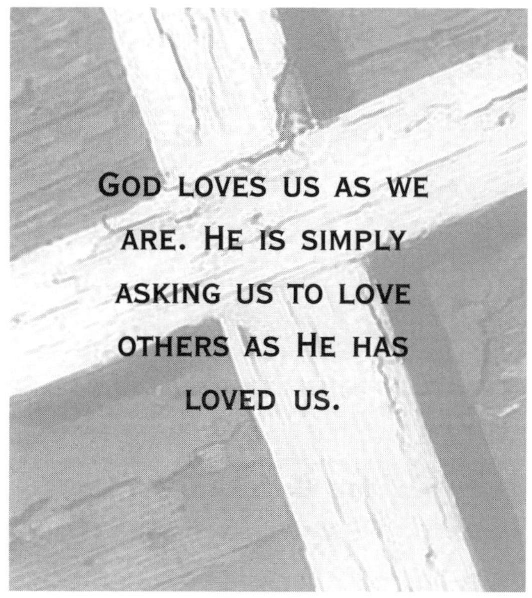

The cost of love is great, but the rewards are far greater. As we die to our own needs and focus upon the needs of others, the greatest fulfillment in this life will begin to be ours. We will become more like Jesus, witnessing the power of His love in our lives. And what greater gift can we give Him than to share His love with others? His love came at the greatest cost of all—His life. As we share His love with others, the warmth of His love will defrost even the coldest heart.

> **Let all that you do be done in love (I Corinthians 16:14).** ■

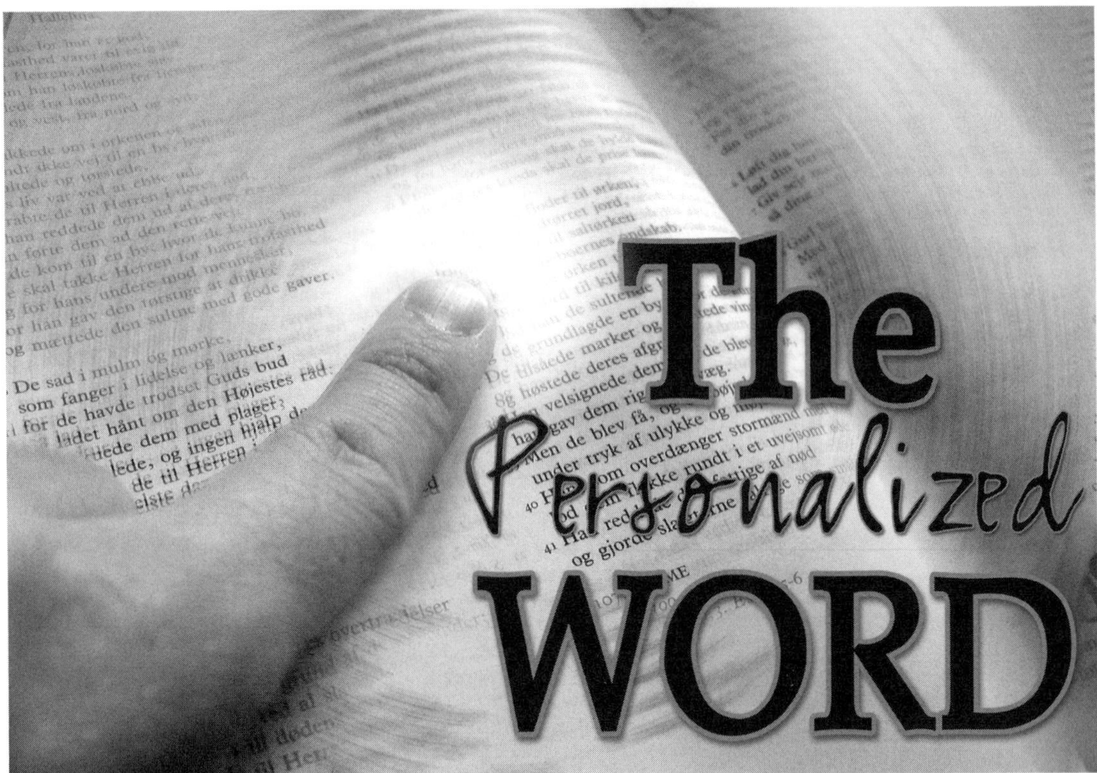

All Scriptures are New King James Version unless otherwise indicated.

by Wade Taylor

And the Word became flesh and dwelt among us...(John 1:14).

The eternal, creative Word became the greatest revelation that God could ever give to man. His Son, the Lord Jesus Christ, was born of a virgin and dwelt among us in condescension, as Jesus of Nazareth, which at that time was considered to be a place of reproach. As He walked the dusty roads of His day, the world saw a visible demonstration of the power and truth of the eternal Word.

That which was from the beginning, which we have heard, which we have seen with our eyes, which we have looked upon, and our hands have handled, concerning the Word of life— that which we have seen and heard we declare to you, that you also may have fellowship with us...(I John 1:1,3).

Each aspect of our lives should be of such quality that the revelation and impartation of the Word, which we hear and receive, will find both expression and fulfillment through us—the Word becoming (our) flesh, a personal reality in our life experience, to be seen and handled by those who surround us.

This will encompass our consecration to the Lord, our walk with Him, our fellowship with the body of believers, of which we are a part, and our relationship to the world in which we live. In each of these areas, that which the Lord has accomplished within us should be evident to others.

In Acts 1:8 Jesus said, **"...you shall be witnesses."** That is, we ourselves are these witnesses. Our growth toward spiritual maturity is nurtured and established through the application of spiritual laws and truths to our lives. Israel saw the deeds of God, but as Moses walked in the ways of God, these things became a part of him. Through the life of Moses, Israel experienced the results of the Lord's revelation to him—only then could they begin to understand.

An Experienced Reality

The objective truth that is set before us in the written Word of God, or in that which is written about the Word of God, must become a practical part of our lives through personal experience before it is really ours. The Word is to become *flesh* (an experienced reality) within our spiritual life experience, as the world both acts and reacts toward us. As we rightly respond to this according to the Word, only then will the world see His life manifested through us. And, they will again marvel and say, **"...No man ever spoke like this Man!" (John 7:46).**

Once our lives are fully committed to the Lord, each decision or choice we make has a higher purpose which transcends its present effect. It is very important for us to understand this so we might rightly view the results of each step that we take toward spiritual maturity.

> **For we are His workmanship, created in Christ Jesus for good works, which God prepared beforehand that we should walk in them (Ephesians 2:10).**

We remember most of our spiritual consecrations because they are made at special times, have a recognizable purpose, and directly affect our spirituality. We value these and hold them as being important spiritual landmarks.

ONCE OUR LIVES ARE FULLY COMMITTED TO THE LORD, EACH DECISION OR CHOICE WE MAKE HAS A HIGHER PURPOSE WHICH TRANSCENDS ITS PRESENT EFFECT.

Along with these, there are the multitudes of seemingly unrelated choices that we are forced to make daily in our lives, which do not appear to us as having any lasting purpose or value. We tolerate these, but think concerning them, "*If I could get past all these mundane things, then I would be able to seek that which has spiritual value and purpose.*"

Decisions

However, the Lord views these seemingly mundane decisions quite differently than we do; these are not merely arbitrary choices that must be made along the pathway of life. From His eternal perspective, varied circumstances are purposely placed in our path so as to provoke us to make decisions concerning them.

The result of these decisions will then become one of the ingredients in the composition of the seed (that which we are becoming) which is being formed by the Lord within our physical frame—our new creation life.

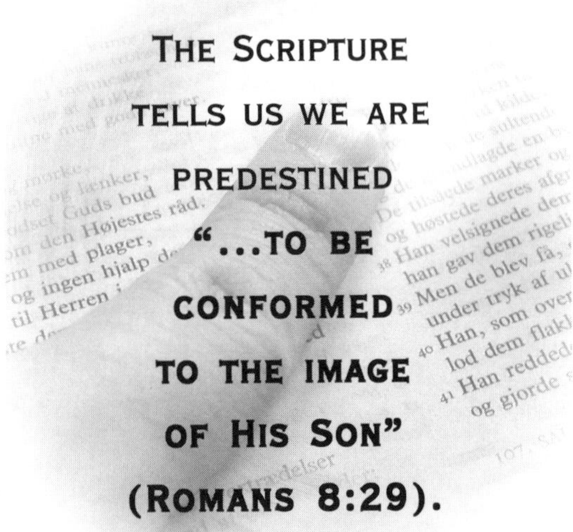

> "**...Behold, a sower** (the Lord) **went forth to sow...**" (the circumstances that require of us a decision or choice) **(Matthew 13:3 KJV).**

The Scripture tells us that we are predestined **"...to be conformed to the image of His Son" (Romans 8:29).** The present development of this **"image"** can be pictured as a *seed* that is being gradually formulated during our span of life. It contains all of the ingredients that are necessary to bring into open manifestation in the age to come, this **"image"** of His Son.

All that is needed for it to be fully revealed is the soil (the atmosphere) of eternity. Once we are there, our life in Him, fully released from the husks of time, will come into full view and we will be measured according to the extent that we have grown into the fullness of His image while here on earth. This can be compared to an apple seed. Every necessary ingredient needed to produce a tree that will grow to maturity and produce apples is contained within this seed. There is nothing that needs to be added to it. All that is required for it to develop into a fully matured tree is the right environment and time.

We often become confused when our spiritual consecrations or decisions, which seemed so outstanding at the time, fade away with no (seemingly to us) lasting consequence. This is because we only see the present effect that these produce. We do not realize that our consecration or decision became an ingredient in the preparation of the "seed" that we are becoming. Nor are we able to see the fully matured tree that will be released from this seed when it enters the environment of eternity.

When the new day dawns, the atmosphere will be present to release the pent-up life that we have become, which is contained within this seed. Only then will it be able to spring forth into its full expression of life. The life that will be manifested from this seed will be the cumulative result of all the ingredients (decisions), both good and bad, that went into its make-up.

Jesus said of this seed, that some **"...fell into good ground, and brought forth fruit, some a hundredfold, some sixtyfold, some thirtyfold" (Matthew 13:8 KJV).** The quality of our consecrations and decisions throughout the span of our life determines which of these gradations will apply to our eternal estate (thirty, sixty, or one hundred).

The most important thing that I can do today is to live in such a way that only the very best ingredients will go into the make-up of this seed that I am becoming. Most of the spiritual consecrations that I make will not presently come to the full outworking of their intended purpose. However, these present spiritual consecrations and decisions are very important, and they have a vital part in the makeup of this seed that will manifest in eternity what we have become in relation to the image of the Lord Jesus Christ.

In eternity, the effect that these consecrations and decisions exercised upon us will develop into their full fruition. There will be ample time then for the outworking of these experiences that present time is not able to accommodate. Much must be accomplished within each one of us in order to bring us to a compatibility with eternity and into a cooperative relationship with the Lord that He both desires and intends.

Ezekiel's Vision

A vision, given to Ezekiel, revealed a man with a four-sided face (see Ezekiel 1:6-10). From one side, he appeared to be as a man, from the second a lion, from the third an ox, and from the fourth an eagle. Each of these views revealed the same man, yet each demonstrated a different quality within his makeup. This vision was repeated to John in Revelation 4:6-7 as four living creatures, who picture the New Testament overcomer.

These four-sided, heavenly views are the result of the outgrowth of a fully developed and matured seed. This understanding of the purpose of the Lord in forming a seed from the cumulative decisions, choices, and experiences of our present life is very important. It will both affect the quality of the decisions we make in our every day experiences, and help us to rightly interpret life. From the Lord's perspective, He will place within our pattern of life experiences all of the circumstances that are necessary so as to enable us to make the decisions which will produce this fully developed seed, which the Lord desires us to become.

THE MOST IMPORTANT THING THAT I CAN DO TODAY IS TO LIVE IN SUCH A WAY THAT ONLY THE VERY BEST INGREDIENTS WILL GO INTO THE MAKEUP OF THIS SEED THAT I AM BECOMING.

A clearer understanding of these things will only be realized in the age to come, when this seed will be manifested as a life, which has become like the **"tree of life,"** bearing all manner of fruit for the healing of the nations (see Revelation 22:2). These will rule with the Lord in the millennial kingdom. Then, we will understand the why of these present difficult experiences which we daily endure, and we will be fully satisfied. ■

Tribute to RICK COMPTON

by Rick Joyner

Rick Compton was a truly gifted man of God, but I also think more importantly, a true friend of God. He was also a friend to Julie and me, as well as many others throughout the body of Christ. He was an inspiration right until his last breath on September 4, 2004. ALS took the life in Rick's body, but there is no question that he lives on, not only in heaven, but in many hearts here on the earth. He left the greatest will of all—a testimony of faith in God and love for God.

I last talked to Rick just a few days before he passed. He could barely speak and struggled for each breath, but his words were clear in both sound and spirit. He said simply that he was trusting the Lord to heal him, but even if He did not, he was excited to soon be able to see Him face to face. He was using his invalid time to pray and to continue being changed into the Lord's nature. I could tell that he was being successful.

Bob Mumford has remarked to me a few times lately how sad it is that so many who accomplish great things die in failure and shame. How desperately we need examples of those who not only run well, but end well. Rick will always be remembered as one who tried to live a life that glorified God, who loved God, and worshiped Him continually. He died well, in possibly the greatest demonstration of faith in his life. When Rick was diagnosed with Lou Gehrig's disease in November 2003, he faced it with great courage. As the disease began to destroy his muscle control and the strength in his hands, he learned to use his feet. Even so, it quickly progressed until he was almost completely paralyzed. However, his mind and heart remained strong right to the end and he never gave up hope. He was not healed of this disease, but he overcame it, and will always be a testimony of God's strength in his weakness and suffering. That too is freedom and deliverance. There is no question that he is now stronger than ever as he joins the great company of witnesses in heaven who are looking down upon us all, and I am sure, cheering us on.

> IF HE DECIDES IT IS TIME TO SEE HIM FACE TO FACE THIS IS GAIN FOR ME. I WILL CONTINUE TO DECLARE "I WILL NOT DIE BUT LIVE AND DECLARE THE WORKS OF THE LORD."

Rick was born a worshiper and dearly loved God, His creation, and His church. He also loved his family. I think he had the purest tenor voice of anyone I have known. It was not just musically pure, but pure in the anointing. When I heard that Rick had passed, I immediately wondered why he and John Hamrick, who I thought had the greatest bass voice, would pass away the same year. There just must be something going on in the heavenly choir! Those two were also good friends and I know they are enjoying each other now. I also know that heaven is enjoying them. I also think heaven owes us at least two first round draft choices for each of them! Rick and John not only had great voices, but they were great people and we will miss them both sorely.

The following is an email I received from Rick just a couple of weeks before he passed. I felt when I read it that it was meant for more than just me.

Rick Joyner

August 15, 2004

THANKS FOR THE NOTE. I REALLY APPRECIATE ALL OF YOUR PRAYERS AND SUPPORT. THE LORD IS AMAZING THROUGH ALL THIS. HE ALLOWS US THE PRIVILEGE OF SHARING IN HIS SUFFERING BUT HE SENDS THE COMFORTER WITH STRENGTH SO THAT IT IS HARDLY A BURDEN AT ALL. HE IS STILL LETTING ME SERVE AND BE HIS WITNESS EVEN FROM THIS PLACE OF GREAT WEAKNESS (I AM TYPING WITH MY TOES). THIS IS HAVING A GREAT EFFECT ON FAMILY, FRIENDS, AND EVEN STRANGERS AS WE STAND IN HIS GOODNESS, MERCY, AND STRENGTH. WE ARE BELIEVING FOR COMPLETE HEALING AND THAT THE LORD HAS SOME PROPHETIC PROMISES THAT HAVE NOT BEEN FULFILLED YET. BUT EVEN IF HE DECIDES IT IS TIME TO SEE HIM FACE TO FACE, THIS IS GAIN FOR ME. I WILL CONTINUE TO DECLARE "I WILL NOT DIE BUT LIVE AND DECLARE THE WORKS OF THE LORD."

YOUR BROTHER AND FRIEND

RICK COMPTON

The House of Joy has established a program for Sally, Rick Compton's wife, called the "Widow's Might." If you would like to contribute toward this fund for Sally, please make checks payable to: The House of Joy, and mail to 2856 Greenbrook Drive, Wendell, North Carolina 27591. All contributions are tax deductible. ■

Love Undo Me Lord

by Tracee Anne Loosle

Love undo me Lord
'Til I'm consumed by only You.
Burn up all the chaff;
Wick away the dross that blocks the view of only You.

Love undo me Lord
'Til I'm filled with only You.
Take this broken vessel;
Seal me in Your fiery flames of holy love in only You.

Love undo me Lord
'Til it's about only You.
Give me a servant's heart;
Fill it up with unselfish love spilling out for only You.

Love undo me Lord
'Til I lay down my life,
Walking in Your righteousness,
Living in Your peace and rest abiding in only You.

Love undo me Lord
'Til I live all for You,
Embraced in the power of the cross,
Revealing eternal life of hope found in only You.

Love undo me Lord
'Til I lay down my rights,
Flowing with love for others,
Faithful to impart the truth about the heart of only You.

Love undo me Lord
'Til you can use my life.
Take away all fears and strife;
Flood me with Your light 'til I'm a beacon for only You.

"I have been crucified with Christ; and it is no longer I who live, but Christ lives in me; and the life which I now live in the flesh I live by faith in the Son of God, who loved me and gave Himself up for me" (Galatians 2:20).

Dealing with the Deadwood

by Steve Thompson

I received an unusual word from the Lord recently. He said "I am going to speak to you at home." Since home is where He speaks to me most frequently, I expected a dramatic visitation or a spectacular prophetic encounter. After waiting for a few weeks for the supernatural event, I discovered that God speaks as much through seemingly natural situations as those we deem supernatural.

While I was still waiting for an extraordinary encounter, I spent significant time developing the property around my home. My house is situated on ten acres of land surrounded mostly by other tracts of undeveloped land. When our building site was initially cleared years ago, a number of large trees were downed but not removed. They were simply pushed away, along with some large boulders, and left between my house and the borders of my property. The trees never rotted because they were locust trees, which actually become harder after they die. I soon forgot about these downed trees because an abundance of plants and even small trees quickly grew up to hide them.

However, as my family has grown over the past five years, I have had to reclaim increasing amounts of the forest to develop a larger yard for playing sports with my children. I had taken as much ground as was possible without dealing with the downed trees and seemingly immoveable boulders. Now, I had no other choice. If I wanted to continue taking ground, I had to confront the pile of rubble. So I began working systematically to remove the deadwood from my property.

The Work

The work was actually easier than I expected, but more time-consuming. By using a small earthmoving machine called a Bobcat, I was able to remove the large trees and stones, and pile the trees in a clearing to be burned later. I moved the stones into a large depression and completed the remaining gaps with fill dirt. The transformation process was slow and steady, which made the changes almost indiscernible to me, although everyone else who saw it was amazed.

Each time it looked as if it would rain, I pushed myself to work long hours, just hoping to get a little more accomplished, but the rain was continually held back.

Some of the trees were so large that they could not be carried—they had to be maneuvered or pushed into a pile. Some of the rocks were so awkward and large that it took a while to find the right angle to scoop them up for removal. Also, there was no way to analyze and plan for removing all of this debris, I just had to start with whatever was moveable and then deal with whatever came next. It turned out to be much more of an art than a science.

One reason I had not confronted this pile of debris before was that the Bobcat is unusable in wet conditions. My free time is so limited that I could not imagine being able to make too much progress before the rain would stop me. Remarkably each time that rain was forecast, it never came. Each time it looked as if it would rain, I pushed myself to work long hours, just hoping to get a little more accomplished, and the rain was continually held back.

Finally, after a few weeks of long, but fulfilling work, I had amassed a gigantic circle of trees, stumps, and underbrush over nine feet high and in some places more than fifty feet in diameter. Obviously, there was a lot more deadwood, underbrush, and stones on my property than I realized. In addition to the pile of deadwood, I had also filled in several large depressions on my land and made them level and smooth. When I finished, I was amazed that the rain had been withheld for so long.

Now I needed wet weather because the only way to ultimately be rid of the deadwood was to burn it. I could not risk starting a fire of this size, unless the ground and surrounding trees were thoroughly soaked with water. After obtaining a burning permit from the county officials, I waited for the wet weather that would protect the rest of the property from the fire. When the rain came and I started the fire, I watched over the next forty-eight hours as the huge pile of deadwood was reduced to a small pile of ashes.

Through every aspect of this project, the Lord spoke to me so naturally and simply that I was almost tempted to reject it as being me. But I soon realized this was the word the Lord had promised to speak to me at home. It was not the dramatic encounter I was expecting, however, it was powerful nonetheless. The Lord revealed this as a current process for many in the church and a crucial reason that the spiritual rain has been withheld.

The Message

We all have deadwood that needs to be dealt with in our lives. The deadwood may be hidden by ground cover, even attractive looking stuff, but ultimately we are affected and restricted by this deadwood. The downed trees, underbrush, boulders, and other stones represent the wrong ideas that we carry about God, ourselves, and one another. We do not carry these concepts consciously, but rather in the recesses of our souls.

The deadwood and stones represent the things that have been moved out of the way in the past, in order for us to build our lives and the place we currently occupy spiritually, emotionally, and professionally. However, these obstacles have never been completely removed. They still linger around the borders of our lives and restrict our vision, limit our perspective, narrow our borders, and provide a habitat for the enemy to harass us.

Anyone who is moving forward in life encounters difficult situations and has to move many obstacles out of the way. Many times the conflict in our souls, between us and others, and our thoughts about God, are not really completely dealt with because of the time constraints and press of life. So we continue moving forward, living life, and these conflicts that occur are never fully dealt with. We notice them at first, but they soon become hidden under the growth of our lives, yet they still remain. But this deadwood must be dealt with. There are three basic areas where we have this deadwood.

The downed trees, underbrush, boulders, and other stones represent the wrong ideas that we carry about God, ourselves, and one another.

First, although God never changes, our perception of Him does. As we mature, our understanding of God changes for the better. However, certain wrong concepts can still plague us—such as the wrong notion that He is easily provoked, impatient, or vindictive. Although we may no longer hold these ideas as part of our theology, they continue lying hidden in our souls and are a breeding ground for the enemy. They can also restrict our vision and pervert our perspective as well.

Second, though God does not change, people can and generally do. Often though, we inadvertently hold people to "moments in time." Though we believe they have changed, our souls still have the "fallen trees of past experience" lying around them. These pieces of deadwood and stone-like obstacles cause us to react to someone based on their past history, instead of their current state. We may have imaginary conversations and arguments with them because of this. If the deadwood of past conflicts in relationships is not dealt with, our current relationships will be negatively affected.

...if we go through the process of identifying and uprooting the deadwood and the stones of wrong thinking about God, others, and ourselves, the results will be amazing.

Third, believe it or not, we can also change. However, this may be the area that most people have the greatest amount of deadwood. Most of us continue harboring inaccurate thoughts and concepts about ourselves. Some of us still see ourselves as we used to be or as others have defined us, and this can also pervert our perspective and hinder our vision. If this is not dealt with we will be bound to our pasts and unable to move forward in life unimpeded, ultimately hindering our faith and God's calling on our lives.

However, if we go through the process of identifying and uprooting the deadwood and the stones of wrong thinking about God, others, and ourselves, the results can and will be amazing. Consider what happened naturally with my property and the applications to our lives are clear.

The Benefits

#1 My Vision Increased

When the weeds, vines, and undergrowth that had sprung up around the downed deadwood were removed, I realized how restricted my vision had become. I had not realized that my vision was limited by the things that grew up around this deadwood. After it was all removed, I could see clearly beyond the borders of my own property.

#2 My Perspective Changed

Amazingly, as the undergrowth was thinned out, each tree and plant that was left stood out more boldly. The landscape that had appeared flat and plain, now came alive visually. Literally the undergrowth arising from the deadwood had given me a bad perspective. Things appeared to be less glorious than they really were. When the deadwood was removed, the beauty of the Lord's creation was restored.

#3 My Borders Were Increased

The borders of my property are established and limited unless I purchase more land. However, the deadwood that had remained kept me from utilizing my property fully. The deadwood and the undergrowth had actually become an artificial border, causing me to live in a narrower place than possible. I was unable to utilize my land fully. When I dealt with the deadwood, my usable borders were increased.

#4 The Snake Habitat was Removed

Although my primary purpose in dealing with the deadwood was taking more ground for my family, there was a secondary motive. Our geographic region is home to three of the four poisonous snake species which inhabit the United States. I have already killed rattlesnakes and copperheads in or near my yard. My secondary purpose in dealing with the deadwood was to reduce the environment suitable for the snake population.

Snakes inhabit downed trees and brush and I prefer my property as "snake free" as possible. While we have to deal with the occasional snake passing through, I certainly do not want a breeding ground for snakes in my yard. Rattlers speak prophetically of those things that rattle us and copperheads speak of the religious spirit. Who needs a breeding ground for anxiety or religious reactions in their life? There is plenty to deal with already, without providing a comfortable place for them.

#5 The Soil Was Renewed

Finally there was another great benefit. Not only did I now have more land that could be developed into a suitable environment for my family, but it became very fruitful land. When the deadwood was burned, the ashes that were left behind from the fire actually helped renew the soil beneath it. These ashes provided balanced and nutritious soil for planting anything that I wanted.

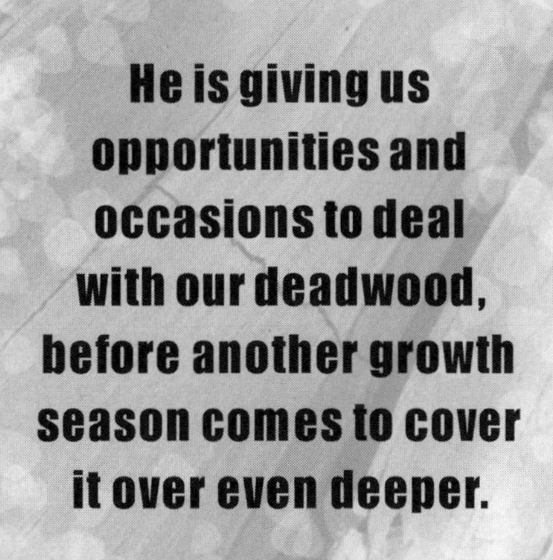

The Application

Some of us have wondered why the rain has been withheld from our lives. My conviction is that God has withheld it *for* us, not *from* us. He is giving us opportunities and occasions to deal with our deadwood, before another growth season comes to cover it over even deeper. The wrong thoughts and concepts that are left over and remain from past experiences will hinder us and make place for the enemy. It behooves us to deal with it while we can.

Additionally, these wrong concepts and thoughts about God, others, and ourselves not only hinder us, they hinder those who are supposed to be recipients of God's grace through us. This is another reason to gather and burn these things during this season. God wants to use us in greater ways, and we need to have these obstacles removed from our lives so we are more fit vessels for His service. The Word of the Lord through Isaiah provides insight and impetus into this process.

> **Go through, go through the gates; Clear the way for the people; Build up, build up the highway; Remove the stones, lift up a standard over the peoples. (Isaiah 62:10).**

This Scripture repeats two phrases twice. **"Go through, go through the gates"** and **"build up, build up the highway."** The process of dealing with our deadwood involves repetition. We must repeatedly give ourselves to the process of forgiving others and taking "every wrong thought captive" about God, ourselves, and others. It is not that difficult, but it is time-consuming. Also, dealing with the deadwood prepares us to be more effective ministers of God's grace to others. This makes a way for the people, not just us.

Now is the time to deal with these past issues. The things that are dead in our lives, but still hanging around, must be gathered up and burned. There is little way to analyze what we must do first, but if we simply begin with the first thing that is apparent, the process will become clear for us as we go. The process is not short and will require that we repeatedly and dedicatedly overcome past issues and thought patterns. However, at the end of this process the only thing that will remain of this deadwood are the ashes that will renew and make our souls more fruitful. ■

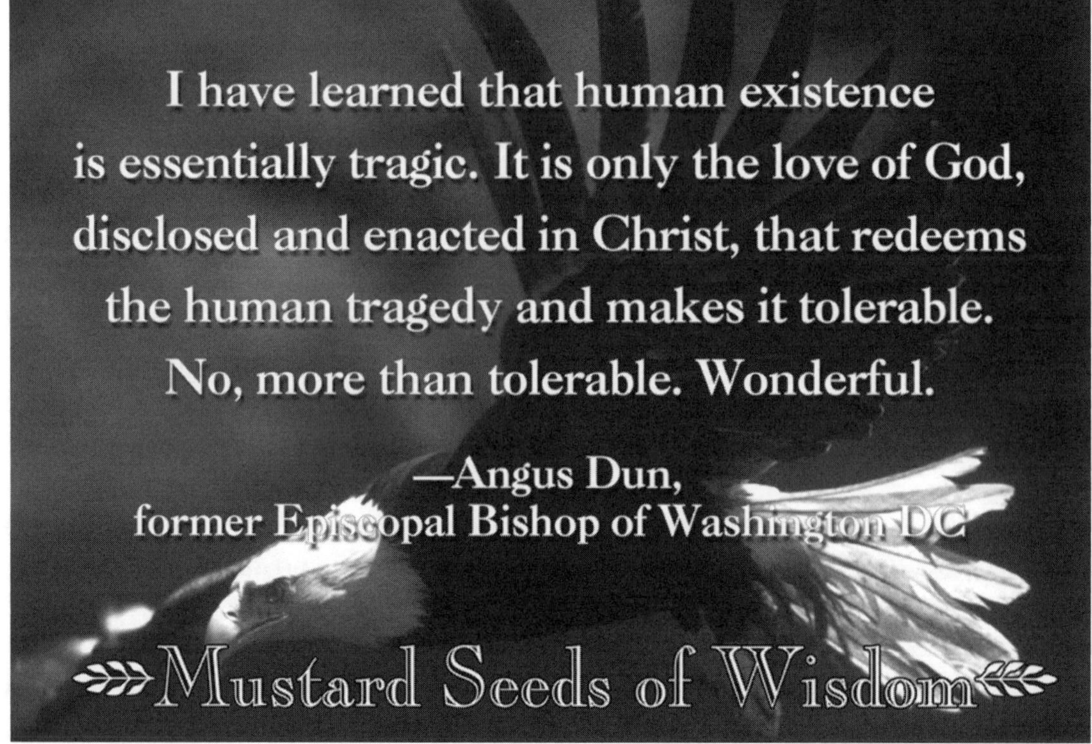

Witnessing Heaven on Earth

by Trevor Tiessen

After these things I looked, and behold, a door standing open in heaven, and the first voice which I had heard, like the sound of a trumpet speaking with me, said, "Come up here, and I will show you what must take place after these things."

Immediately I was in the Spirit; and behold a throne was standing in heaven, and One sitting on the throne. (Revelation 4:1-2).

The encounter that the apostle John experienced on the island of Patmos was not an isolated incident. The Lord wants us to have this type of experience as well. He desires to reveal more of Himself and His kingdom to us and invites us to "**come up here**" and see it.

In December 2003, the Lord revealed Himself to me in a way I had never experienced before. My life was changed and it has brought me closer to the Lord.

In the Spirit

During one of our Sunday services, the youth prayed for people in our congregation to be caught up in the Spirit. Not long before, the youth in our church had recently had this experience. During that service, I was one of the people for whom they prayed.

With my eyes closed and my hands in the air, the first thing I saw was something like tinsel falling off my arms. Instinctively, I knew these were chains falling off—mindsets that were keeping me bound. To me they were like the anchor chains of the Titanic, something that was impossible to break. However, to the Lord it was just tinsel.

After that, I started to fly straight up at an incredible speed (this was happening in the Spirit, not physically). I could hear the sound of the wind going by me. A friend of mine happened to walk by and put her hand on my shoulder and said, "He is going up like a rocket." This statement stunned me, reinforcing the reality of what was happening.

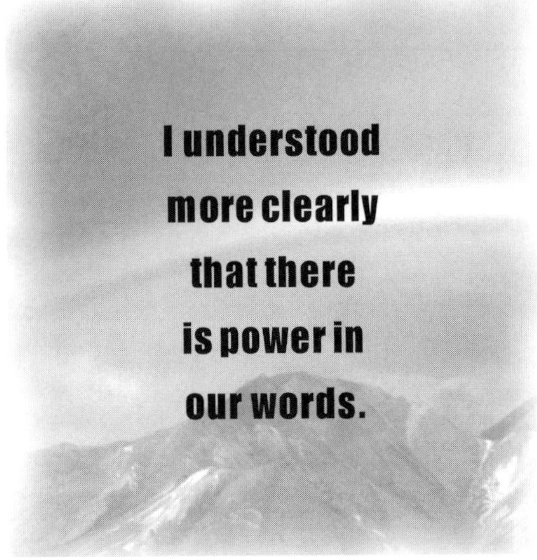

I continued flying up until I was in outer space where I saw a golden throne. It was the size of the earth itself. I could see that the throne was actually made up of thousands and thousands of smaller thrones.

I looked down on one of the armrests and saw rows and rows of thrones. People I knew were sitting on thrones next to each other. They were laughing and having fun. I saw the pastor of our Charlotte congregation there, but he was not sitting on a throne. He was walking through the isles making sure that everyone else was sitting on their thrones.

There was a throne there for me and I sat down on it. I felt a little awkward and unsure, but it was amazing. I had a very real sense of power and it was humbling. I felt I had to be careful about what I said because I knew that whatever I spoke would come to pass. I did not have to pray; I could speak a command and it would happen.

In the following Scriptures, Paul reveals that we have been raised up with Christ in the heavenly realm.

> **But God, being rich in mercy, because of His great love with which He loved us,**
>
> **even when we were dead in our transgressions, made us alive together with Christ (by grace you have been saved),**
>
> **and raised us up with Him and seated us with Him in the heavenly places, in Christ Jesus (Ephesians 2:4-6).**

What I saw was a real time picture of what was happening in the Spirit. I was able to see in the Spirit for the first time that I was truly seated with Christ. I had authority with the most powerful Being in the universe and I felt it! I understood more clearly that there is power in our words. It is not only our prayers that matter, but also everything we say. We have the power to release life or death in anything we speak. This was very humbling and caused me to consider my own words.

After the experience, I felt numb, but my senses were not dull; they were sharp. As I looked around, I was already seeing some things that could have irritated me, but I felt a spiritual barrier protecting me from offense. I did not have to tolerate or forgive anyone because I could not feel any offense. Jesus explains to us that **"...the kingdom of God does not come with signs to be observed *or* with visible display, nor will people say, Look! Here [it is]! or, See, [it is] there! For behold, the kingdom of God is within you [in your hearts] and among you [surrounding you]" (Luke 17:20-21 AMP)**. I truly felt surrounded and shielded by His presence.

The feeling eventually subsided after this experience, but I felt an increase in faith and hope and saw the Lord in a way that I had not previously. Tasting His goodness has changed me permanently.

Paul's Experience

Heaven is not only a place that we go when we die, but also a place we can visit and experience in this life. Jesus Himself prayed, **"Your kingdom come. Your will be done, on earth as it is in heaven." Matthew 6:10.** We have been invited to experience heaven on earth by the Lord. The kingdom of God does not come with our observation, but the kingdom of God is within us. We can witness the reality of heaven with the eyes of our hearts.

> **I know a man in Christ who fourteen years ago—whether in the body or out of the body I do not know, God knows—was caught up to the third heaven.**
>
> **And I know that this man—whether in the body or away from the body I do not know, God knows—was caught up into paradise, and he heard utterances beyond the power of man to put into words, which man is not permitted to utter (II Corinthians 12:2-4 AMP).**

The experiences that the enemy tries to lure us with are only a counterfeit of the true spiritual encounters the Lord wants us to have with Him.

So, the apostle John was not the only one to speak of these experiences. Paul, speaking of himself, describes how he was caught up to the third heaven. His encounter was such that he was not sure if he was still in his body or not. The church generally labels "out of body experiences" as occult or demonic, but here we see that Paul had this very experience. The experiences that the enemy tries to lure us with are only a counterfeit of the true spiritual encounters the Lord wants us to have with Him.

The Lord does not want His people to be suspicious of the supernatural, but to walk in the supernatural. He desires for us to meet with Him. As Christians, we should be more comfortable in the realm of the Spirit than in this earthly realm. The earth serves as our temporary accommodation, but heaven is our home.

The Economy of Heaven

In a later experience, I was in the Spirit where the Lord showed me what was in heaven. I saw a number of things I did not expect to see.

One of the things I saw were many rows of huge cylindrical storage tanks. I asked the Lord what these tanks were for. He said, *"Fuel for the elect."* It was gasoline for vehicles owned by believers—a supernatural supply that could be accessed by faith. The Lord then held up an American one dollar bill and told me, *"This will give you access to the world's supply, but faith will give you access to My supply."*

While in the Spirit, I also saw parking lots of cars. Some models dated back to the 1930s, 40s, and 50s. I wondered why these vehicles were there, since I understood no one in heaven needed a car. Then I realized that they were never accessed by faith, so they were still there. Believers from those generations could have accessed this provision by faith, but did not do so.

I also had the sense that there is provision in heaven for technology that does not even exist yet. There is a supply in heaven already waiting for a future generation. Even though this technology does not exist here yet, it is already in heaven. The kingdom of God is timeless and eternal. The provision of heaven is not subject to our timeline on earth.

No one in heaven needs cars, gasoline, or earthly provisions, but they are needed here on earth. By entering into the Spirit, we can see with the eyes of faith what the Lord has intended for us. But it is more than just seeing His provision for us; the Lord desires that we walk and live with Him in the Spirit.

Summary

The Lord is calling us to come up to heaven. He wants to not only reveal what is in heaven, but Who is in heaven. The Lord dearly wants us to have encounters with Him, often. He wants us to see Him as He really is. In everything I experienced, I felt His love and compassion for me. There are some things I could not even include in this article because they were so specific and personal—this is just how He feels toward us. Rather than receiving our encouragement from our circumstances, which can change with the weather, let us seek our hope and encouragement from heaven, an eternal kingdom that cannot be shaken. ■

END TIME PROPHETIC PRAYER

by Morris Cerullo

God is raising up a mighty prayer army of spiritual warriors who will be used mightily in the Spirit to fulfill His purposes in this end-time hour. This prayer army is not the work of a man or the result of an organization. He is going to send you forth into your churches...into your homes... into your cities...into your villages...into the uttermost part of the world! God is anointing you.

He is placing a mantle of intercession upon you. You are not going to be led or directed by man, but by the Spirit of the living God.

You are going to enter a new realm of the Spirit where your prayers are divinely energized, divinely directed, divinely motivated, and released into the heavenlies.

As your prayers ascend up before God, they will be a sweet-smelling savor in His nostrils, and as a result of your prayers, He will commission and send forth warrior angels to war against and destroy the strongholds of the rulers, powers, and principalities of the kingdom of darkness that have established strongholds over your cities, villages, and nations.

As you enter this new realm of the Spirit through prayer, God will open your understanding and reveal to you the secrets of the enemy—his plans, strategies, and schemes that he has devised to frustrate and hinder the gospel of Jesus Christ from penetrating the hearts and minds of the people.

Armed with this knowledge, you will be prepared to take your position of authority in the heavenlies to speak forth and declare His judgments upon the earth...to declare His will...to declare His victories!

This mighty army of spiritual warriors God is raising up will be led and directed by His almighty hand. He will send you forth by His Spirit to cover your villages, cities, and nations with prayer. This is a high and holy calling and requires a full submission of your will...your life...your single-hearted dedication and commitment to God.

You must have a new vision of the purposes that God desires for prayer in this end-time hour. The old ways, the ways of tradition and formality are not sufficient for this hour and they will not succeed! God is saying: Your prayers must become an extension of My thoughts, My purposes, My plans. You must first learn to know My heart by waiting before Me in My presence. As I reveal the secrets of My heart to you, you will know how to pray prayers that will penetrate and dispel the darkness.

When you know My heart, you will have divinely energized prayers, for your words will proceed forth from My heart, and as you pray, your words will release My power to fulfill My desires. I will give you a hearing ear so that you will hear My voice clearly. From this day forward, I call you into account for the prayers you offer unto Me or speak in My name or in My behalf. Do not rely upon your limited understanding.

I have placed my Holy Spirit within you to direct your prayers. Yield yourself fully to My Spirit. Do not trust in your own wisdom, but draw from My Spirit within you. Die to yourself and My Spirit will be released within you and He will pray through you. As My Spirit is released within you, you will be able to confront the enemy in My power and authority! You will do great exploits! You will launch out into new spiritual territories to take the victories God has already given you. ■

Used by permission. Contact Morris Cerullo World Evangelism for more information at www.mcwe.com

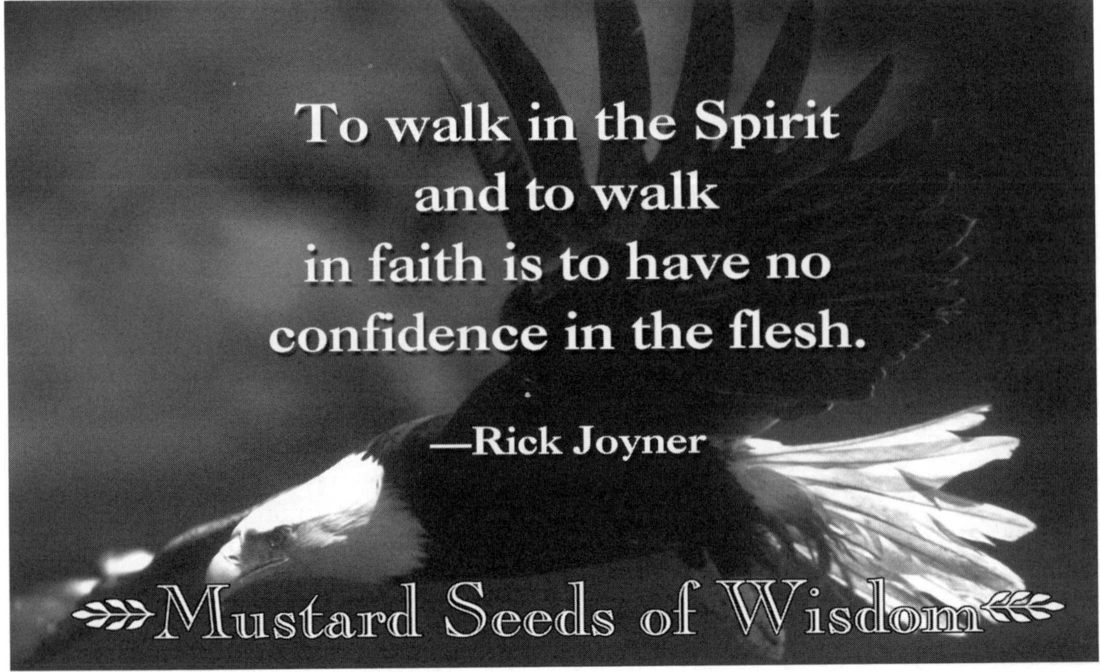

The Call for Courage

by Rick Joyner

"And you will be hearing of wars and rumors of wars; see that you are not frightened, for those things must take place, but that is not yet the end" (Matthew 24:6).

We must consider that the Lord says this right after the verse in which He exhorts us not to be deceived. Because war is the worst of all judgments, the most terrible of all conditions in which we can be caught, it is hard not to think that when war comes upon us it is the end of the world. In almost every war Christians have indeed felt that it was the end of the world. Just as He warns us here, our fear can mislead us and cause us to think this.

Immediately after the attacks on September 11, I was amazed at how so many major newspapers and news organizations called seeking a biblical or prophetic interpretation of what had happened. I was surprised by how many had at least a sense that this was somehow a harbinger of the end of the age, even though they did not know why. I do not ever remember hearing the Lord mentioned so often on the news and with such respect. Attendance records were broken in churches across the country. This openness to the Lord may not have lasted long, but it was dramatic for a time, and many people did at least become more spiritually aware.

Even so, we will be having many wars and many rumors of wars, compelling many to wrongly think it is the end. Even though this may present many opportunities for the gospel, we do not want to be misled into thinking that these things represent the end, and we do not want to use them to mislead others.

Many have already heard "it's the end" so many times that they are hardened against this message now. Regardless of this, at some point it will indeed be the end. So how will we know? How will we warn others when it is? Almost every generation of Christians at some point thought that they were the last generation of the age, and consequently they were all deceived on this point. One way I think we can help protect ourselves against this same deception is for our message of the end to not be overly focused on the end, but on the new beginning that it is. Our message is the ultimate message of hope—the King is coming! Our message is not a message of doom—it is a message of a new beginning!

Our message is the ultimate message of hope—the King is coming!

For too long the church has been so focused on the end, with its message so focused on doom, that we have not used the most powerful message that we were given—the gospel of the kingdom. This is the greatest message of hope the world has ever heard, and it will be preached throughout the world when the world needs it the most and is ready to hear it. I was sorry when the September 11 attacks came that I was not more prepared for the opportunities for the gospel which came my way. I do not want to be so unprepared again. But I still do not want to use fear, especially fear not based on truth, to compel people to come to the Lord. Such conversions are usually too superficial to last.

There is also a factor that we need to understand about war. When I was in the Navy, because I was stationed for a time on a base where everyone was required to be a part of the ground defense force, I had to go through basic Marine Corps infantry training. A good part of this training was learning basic battle strategies and tactics. We were taught over and over how important a good battle plan was. Then, to our amazement, we were told that rarely did a battle ever follow the plan. In fact, most battles are semi-controlled chaos. We were told simply that the one who could deal with confusion best would have the best chance to both survive and win the battle. Fear and confusion usually cause people to shut down and become passive, so the one who overcomes this and takes action, wins.

War is chaos and confusion even for those who are well trained for it. It is far worse for civilians who are caught in it. This is why the Lord tells His people in the exhortation above to "not be afraid." We should not be surprised by these things, and we should be better prepared for them than any soldier. Regardless of what is happening in this world, if our lives have been built on the kingdom that cannot be shaken, we will not be shaken by what goes on in the world.

We were not redeemed and then left on the earth just to be blessed and have a good time. Every Christian who is still here is here for one purpose—to be a part of proclaiming the gospel of the kingdom. Neither should we be shut down because of any antichrist, as Daniel 11:31-32 declares:

> **"And forces from him** (the antichrist) **will arise, desecrate the sanctuary fortress, and do away with the regular sacrifice. And they will set up the abomination of desolation.**
>
> **"And by smooth words he will turn to godlessness those who act wickedly toward the covenant, *but the people who know their God will display strength and take action*."**

So, when **"wars and rumors of wars"** come we must take heed to the Lord's command to "be not afraid." Fear will not only cloud our thinking, leading us into deception, but it will also cause us to miss some of the greatest opportunities for the gospel. We must gird ourselves for action. The more confusing it gets, the more imperative it will be for us to be strong and bold.

Regardless of whether this coming war is the very end or not, war will be the end for many people. If we find ourselves in any such conflict, we are there for a reason, and the reason is to take action. Christians, who are assured of eternal life, should always be the most courageous in the midst of danger. For this reason the Lord tells us in Revelation 21:7-8:

> **"He who overcomes shall inherit these things, and I will be his God and he will be My son.**
>
> **"But for the cowardly and unbelieving and abominable and murderers and immoral persons and sorcerers and idolaters and all liars, their part will be in the lake that burns with fire and brimstone, which is the second death."**

Fear will not only cloud our thinking, leading us into deception, but it will also cause us to miss some of the greatest opportunities for the gospel.

Cowards have their portion with the unbelievers and even with the **"abominable and murderers..."** Not having courage is not an option for the Christian. If we do not have courage in the midst of these times it is because we do not really believe. But for those who do rise up to overcome, He will prove to be our God, and we will be shown to be His sons. ■

The 2004 Graduating class of the Comenius School for Creative Leadership

The 2004 graduating class of CSCL is certainly one that will never be forgotten. They set a new standard for the pursuit of God and godly character, as well as academic excellence which I am confident will be an inspiration to many who follow them.

Rick Joyner

At the beginning of the 2003-2004 school year, our senior class under the guidance of our Vice-Principal, Mrs. Woods, met with Bob Jones. This trip changed their lives. Bob Jones commissioned them to go and lay hands on people and pray for them. They did. They first laid hands on everyone in the school and then they prayed for the entire church at Morningstar's Charlotte fellowship. Next, they went to other churches in Charlotte and throughout North Carolina, sharing their testimonies and praying for every person who wanted prayer. Then they traveled to other states and did the same thing. I traveled with them to Kentucky and saw people's lives transformed as they laid hands on them. We heard testimony after testimony of people both young and old having incredible experiences with God as these students prayed for them.

In the midst of this, God spoke and told them to change their senior trip from Hawaii to Australia and New Zealand and to go and pray for the churches over

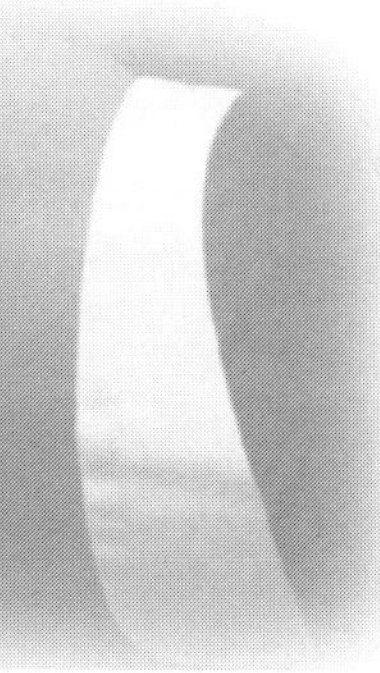

They spoke to many churches, prayed for hundreds of people, and ignited a fire that is still spreading there over six months later.

there. So in faith they raised more than $40,000, and in early spring they traveled south to Australia and New Zealand. They spoke to many churches, prayed for hundreds of people, and ignited a fire that is still spreading there over six months later. It was an amazing year for these seniors and they did it all while pursuing excellence in their academics. In fact, as a group they received more than $200,000 in scholarships to some of the best colleges in the state. As a group, they dedicated their final year of school to pursuing God, achieving incredible things.

The Comenius School for Creative Leadership formed nearly six years ago with an aim of raising up leaders who would be equipped both spiritually and academically. We aim to give our students the opportunities to not only see ministry, but to do ministry. We want our students to not only learn about leadership, but to actually begin being leaders both in the school and outside. Over the past years, we have seen some great leaders raised up from among our students and we have many alumni doing very well in colleges and abroad. The senior class of 2003-2004 was one of the first graduating classes to really take up the challenge as a group, wanting to see the power of God move through them in their final year of school. They had a great year and were changed dramatically as they went out, but above all their hearts were to see the next years' seniors go further. The senior class of 2003-2004 has raised up a standard.

Nathan Plowman
CSCL Principal

We aim to give our students the opportunities to not only see ministry, but to do ministry.

2004 CSCL Graduation Speech

As I stand here on Graduation Day, I am thinking about the journeys which have led each of us to this place.

We stand before you as friends, as family, and as a team. Within us we contain the anthropologist, events planner, musician, artist, writer, doctor, teacher, baker, and businessmen and women of tomorrow. But more importantly, we are the adventurers, chasers, and leaders. We have gone to the end of the earth and come back to share our story and for that, no matter where our journey may now take each of us, we will always stand together—on the forefront of this battle.

Who could have foreseen the adventures we have had? One year ago, twelve people entered their senior year, each one pursuing their own goals. Who would have known that our simple plans, graduation, and senior class trip to Hawaii would be so shaken? No longer would Hawaii fulfill our call, but an even greater miracle would have to do. New Zealand and Australia were too far away, there was no money, and no one really thought that we could do it (except for a few, you know who you are). Yet, here we stand before you as overcomers of jet lag, culture shock, and New Zealand beef. Our testimony is in our actions, but our change is forever in our hearts.

If you would have spoken to me at the beginning of the last school year, you would have found a different person. I think it is safe to say this about all my fellow graduates. I began last year with the hope of keeping my grades up and getting into college, but it seems the Lord had bigger plans for all of us. He sent us on an adventure that has ruined us for life and we will never be the same. We have learned to chase after the Lord's promises; we have learned that faith is about jumping without looking down; and we have learned that the impossible is never out of reach.

Strength lies in the aftermath of our quest and we are now able to face the unknown of tomorrow drawing from where we have been and who we have become.

To my friends: May you never forget who you are; may you never forget where you came from; may you always jump without looking down; may you always chase the Lord's promises and, may you always be ruined for life. ■

Courtney Blake, 2004 CSCL Graduate

We have learned to chase after the Lord's promises; we have learned that faith is about jumping without looking down; and we have learned that the impossible is never out of reach.

All Scripture quotations are taken from the King James Version.

by Charles Spurgeon

Lord, we are longing to draw near to You. May Your Spirit draw us near. We come by the way of Christ our Mediator. We could not approach You, O God, if it were not for Him, but in Him we come boldly to the throne of heavenly grace (see Hebrews 4:16). Nor can we come without thanksgiving—thanksgiving from the heart, such as the tongue can never express. You have chosen us from before the foundation of the world, and this wellspring of mercy sends forth streams of lovingkindness never ceasing. Because we were chosen, we have been redeemed with precious blood. Bless the Lord! We have been called by the Holy Spirit out of the world, and we have been led to obey that wondrous call that has quickened and renewed us, made us the people of God, and given us adoption into the divine family. Bless the Lord!

Our hearts want to pause as we remember the greatness of each one of Your favors, and we want to say, **"Bless the LORD, O my soul: and all that is within me, bless his holy name" (Psalm 103:1).** When we consider our utter unworthiness before conversion, and our great faultiness since, we cannot help but admire the riches of abounding grace that God has manifested to us unworthy ones. Bless the Lord!

When we think of all that You have promised to give, which our faith embraces as being really ours since the covenant makes it sure, we do not know how to proclaim abundantly enough the memory of Your great goodness. We want to make our praises equal to our expectations and our expectations equal to Your promises. We can never rise so high. We give to You, however, the praise of our entire being.

Unto Jehovah, the God of Abraham, the God of Isaac, and the God of Jacob, the Creator of the world, the Redeemer of men, unto Jehovah be glory forever and ever, and let all His people praise Him. **"Let the redeemed of the LORD say so, whom he hath redeemed from the hand of the enemy" (Psalm 107:2).**

MAY EVERY CHILD OF YOURS HAVE HIS CONSCIENCE PURGED FROM DEAD WORKS TO SERVE THE TRUE AND LIVING GOD.

O Lord, Your works praise You, but Your saints bless You. This will be our heaven—our heaven of heavens eternally—to praise and magnify the great and ever blessed God. This day may many men and women break forth and say with the Virgin Mary, **"My soul doth magnify the Lord, and my spirit hath rejoiced in God my Savior" (Luke 1:46–47).** This day may there go up sweet incense of praise laid privately by holy hands upon the altar of God. May the place be filled with the smoke of it, not perhaps to the consciousness of every one, but to the acceptance of God, who will smell a sweet savor of rest in Christ, and then in the praises of His people in Him.

But, Lord, when we praise You, we have to fold the wing. We have to cover the face and cover the feet and stand before You to worship in another fashion, for we confess that we are evil, evil in our nature. Though renewed by sovereign grace, Your people cannot speak of being clean, being rid of sin. There is sin that dwells in us that is our daily plague. O God, we humble ourselves before You. We ask that our faith may clearly perceive the blood of the atonement and the covering of the perfect righteousness of Christ. May we come afresh, depending alone on Jesus. "I, the chief of sinners am, but Jesus died for me." May this be our one hope, that Jesus died and rose again, and that for His sake we are **"accepted in the beloved" (Ephesians 1:6).**

May every child of Yours have his conscience purged from dead works to serve the true and living God. May there be no cloud between us and our heavenly Father—not even a mist, not even the morning mist that is soon gone. May **"we walk in the light, as he** [God] **is in the light ..." (I John 1:7).** May our fellowship with the Father and with His Son, Jesus Christ, be unquestionable. May it be fuel. May it fill us with joy. May it be a most real fact this day. May we enjoy it to the full, knowing whom we have believed, knowing who is our Father, knowing who it is that dwells in us, even the Holy Spirit.

Take away from us everything that might hinder our delighting ourselves in God. May we come to God this day with supreme joy. May we speak of Him as **"God, my exceeding joy," my own God is He" (see Psalm 43:4).** O God, give us a sense of belonging in You. May we come near to You, having no doubt and nothing whatsoever that would spoil the beautiful simplicity of a childlike faith that looks up into the great face of God and says, **"Our Father which art in heaven ..." (Matthew 6:9).**

There are those who have never repented of sin and have never believed in Christ, and consequently the wrath of God abides on them. They are living without God, living in darkness. O God, in Your great mercy, look upon them. They do not look at You, but may You look at them. May the sinner see his sin and mourn, see His Savior and accept Him, see himself saved, and go on his way rejoicing. Father, grant us this.

Once more we pray that You would bless Your church. Lord, quicken the spiritual lives of Your believers. You have given to Your church great activity, for which we thank You. May that activity be supported by a corresponding inner life. Do not let us get busy here and there with Martha, and forget to sit at Your feet with Mary (see Luke 10:39–42). Lord, restore to Your church the love of strong doctrine. May Your truth yet prevail. Purge out from among Your church those who would lead others away from the truth as it is in Jesus, and give back the old power and something more. Give us Pentecost—yes, many Pentecosts in one—and may we live to see Your church shine forth as clear as the sun, as fair as the moon, and as **"terrible as an army with banners" (Song of Solomon 6:4).**

God, grant that we may live to see better days. But if perilous times should come in these last days, make us faithful. Raise up in England, raise up in Scotland, men who will hold the truth firmly as their fathers did. Raise up in every country where there has been a faithful church, men who will not let the ship drift upon the rocks. O God of the judges, You who did raise up first one and then another when the people went astray from God, raise up for us still (for our Joshuas are dead) Deborahs, Baraks, Gideons, Jephthahs, and Samuels, who will maintain for God His truth and defeat the enemies of Israel. Lord, look upon Your church in these days. Lord, revive us. Lord, restore us. Lord, give power to Your Word again so that Your name may be glorified in all the earth.

MAY THE SINNER SEE HIS SIN AND MOURN, SEE HIS SAVIOR AND ACCEPT HIM, SEE HIMSELF SAVED, AND GO ON HIS WAY REJOICING.

Remember the church of God in this land in all its various phases and portions, and pour out Your Spirit upon it. Remember the multitude of Your people across the sea in America; prosper them and bless them with Your increase. Wherever You have a people, may Jesus dwell with them and reveal Himself to His own for Christ's sake, to whom be glory with the Father and with the Holy Spirit, forever and ever. Amen. ■

This article is an excerpt from Charles H. Spurgeon's book, ***Prayer****, pages 85-90, copyright 1995; publisher Whitaker House (www.whitakerhouse.com). Used by permission.*

by Rick Joyner

The following is a rewrite of a series of articles I did a few years ago which I felt then had the potential to be some of the most important prophetic writings I have ever done. Much of this came in the same way as the visions I wrote about in ***The Final Quest*** *series, even though they are looking back at history more than looking ahead into the future. However, these articles look back at the most important time in man's history that there will ever be—the time when God walked the earth.*

This is not just a reprint of what I wrote before, but the laying of a more comprehensive foundation that I expect to build upon in each edition of ***The Morning Star Journal*** *for the next few years.*

PART I

Andrew forced himself to look directly into the piercing eyes of John the Baptist as he waited expectantly for the answer. He had never seen John this way before. He was the most intense man he had ever known, but now he seemed distracted, mentally far away. Finally, Andrew asked him again.

"What happened at the river today?"

The Baptist turned away for a moment to collect his thoughts before looking back at his young disciple, and then he apologized,

"I'm sorry. What did you say?"

His disciples had never witnessed this type of courtesy in John before, and it made them even more uncomfortable. It had been an extraordinary day. Something both frightening and confusing had happened that morning, and now John seemed as if he were a different person. It seemed as if his great fire had been quenched.

Now there was a softness, even a kindness in John. He had never been an intentionally mean person, but he was so intense that he continually trampled the feelings of everyone around him. Now he seemed to be almost sensitive, though very distracted.

"Who was that man you baptized this morning?" Andrew continued at the insistence of the other disciples. "And whose Son is He? We heard a voice say that this was His Son, but we did not see anyone where the voice seemed to come from. We could tell that you heard it, too. Who said it? We could not see anyone, and we have never heard a voice like that."

That morning, as was their custom, John preached to the people while his disciples were baptizing them. Then John stopped and began watching them. Suddenly he jumped up and approached a man who had been patiently waiting in line. Because of the clamor of the people, many of whom were wailing under the weight of their sins, they could not hear what John had said to the man. Then, John personally baptized this one Man, a thing which he rarely did anymore. This had gotten the attention of his disciples. A strange voice, which seemed to come right out of the air, had called this Man His Son. Everyone seemed to hear it and started looking around for who had spoken, but there was no one on the banks or hills above them. This created a mild stirring throughout the entire crowd. When they looked back at John, he was all alone. He walked off without saying anything to anyone.

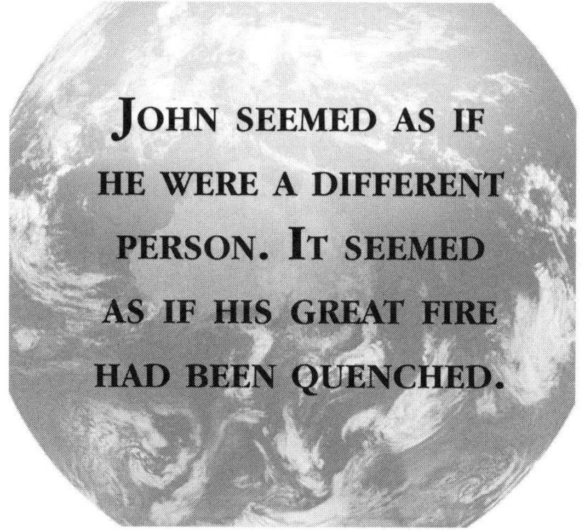

What had started off as a very good day for their work became charged with a strange feeling that came over everyone. John's preaching that morning had been particularly strong and had greatly moved the people to repentance. Then this happened and John just left. Gradually the people began to leave too. It had been one of their biggest crowds yet, and they left in some confusion. This was not good, and the disciples were concerned.

When John returned, he did not seem like himself. This finally compelled his disciples to approach him and ask what this was all about. Because John was such an aloof person, it took courage for even his closest disciples to question him. Even when they had been distraught by the way he offended some of the nobles and priests, they held their peace. But now they felt that something very strange had happened, and they had to have some answers. Finally, the Baptist began to focus on them and spoke, not with confusion but with great joy in his voice.

"...THE KING HIMSELF STOOD RIGHT IN OUR MIDST TODAY. HE WAS THE ONE I BAPTIZED WHEN YOU HEARD THE VOICE OF GOD."

"Friends, this was the day that I was born for. I saw the Lamb of God. He asked me to baptize Him. Now my job is done and my time here will soon end. I have finished my course. Now He must increase, but I must decrease."

Though the Baptist obviously had great joy in this, these words hit his disciples like hammers. They hardly heard the part about the Lamb of God or the momentous statement that this had been the day that John was "born for." What jolted them more than anything was hearing that his time was almost up, and that he was finished with what he had been given to do. It seemed as if everything was just beginning. All of Judea was now coming out to hear him, and even many of the priests were now coming to be baptized. They had the attention of the entire nation. How could they stop now? John had been talking about the kingdom being at hand. How could he talk of his time being up? John gazed around at each of his disciples with what looked like compassion, and continued.

"Friends, truly the kingdom is at hand. Please listen to me. The King Himself stood right in our midst today. He was the One I baptized when you heard the voice of God."

"The voice of God!" several exclaimed together. "Was that the voice of God we heard?"

"It was. That was the Father saying, 'This is My beloved Son, with whom I am well pleased.' Today I baptized the Son of God. He is the One who existed from the beginning. He is now walking among us. These are the days of the great wonders of God. He has come to us Himself, in His Son. He walks among us as a Man. He has come in humility like a lamb, but I tell you, He is the great King. He will set up a kingdom that has no end. This is the One who I was sent to prepare the way for. He was here today!"

John paused as if he would drift back into the faraway state he had been in for many hours. Andrew quickly begged him to continue, asking him once again about the voice.

"That voice was the Father. Even so, many of you are going to witness more glorious things in the times to come. The One about whom the angels have told me is now taking His place among us. My time is up, but His is just beginning. I leave fulfilled because I have seen Him. I saw the heavens open and the Holy Spirit descend...and He remained on Him. He is the One who will baptize you with the Holy Spirit and with fire!"

Then the Baptist stood up and walked off by himself. His disciples knew that he was going to pray and that he would talk no more until the next day. They watched him until he was out of sight and then they began talking among themselves.

"What does all of this mean?" one of them asked, looking at Andrew.

"All along John said that he was just preparing the way for another," Andrew replied. "He did say that the one he was waiting for was much greater than he. I thought he was talking about the Messiah—but the Son of God! God walking among us as a Man! But we all heard the voice, and there was no one around who could have spoken that way. This is hard to understand. Maybe tomorrow he will tell us more."

"But what does it mean that John's time is up?" asked another, without trying to hide his emotions. "We have been through so much together. We have stood by him through everything. He has probably offended every powerful person in the country by now, and we are known to be his disciples. What will we do if he leaves? Where would he go? Where will we go? We know that he is a prophet sent from God. We cannot give up everything that we have risked so much to build. In spite of the rage of so many of the leaders, the whole nation is listening to us now."

"HAVE YOU NOT HEARD WHAT THE BAPTIST SAID? HE SAID THE SON OF GOD WAS RIGHT HERE TODAY!"

For the first time John, the son of Zebedee, spoke up with a deep, yet controlled, passion.

"Have you not heard what the Baptist said? He said the Son of God was right here today! And we all heard the voice. It had to be God; no one else was around. We have all known great times with the Baptist. Our hearts have been plowed, but in a way that gave us hope. The nation is stirred because God is speaking to His people again. We have been most privileged to be this close to him but it seems that something even more wonderful is now here. We must not look back, but forward. The prophet said that the Son of God was here today; I intend to find Him tomorrow."

The faces of some betrayed their skepticism, but John continued. "I love the Baptist. I love him more than my own father. He is our father in many ways. I am so thankful to have been able to be so close to a real prophet sent from God. If this is the Son of God, He must also be the Messiah. If He is, we must now follow Him. The Baptist himself said that his time was up, but the time of this One who is the Son of God is just beginning."

The power of his vision and resolve swept up even the most learned and powerful into a new and living hope in the God of Israel.

Except for Andrew, the others could not consider leaving John. They had too much invested in him and his message. The group began to break up. In just a few hours they had gone from feeling ready to take over the nation to having serious doubts. Feelings of the impending end of something wonderful started to come over them like a fog coming in from the sea. For John and Andrew, a new and greater hope was just awakening.

This little band of John's disciples, composed mostly of common folk, had risen to the pinnacle of spiritual influence throughout Judea. It was a place they had never dreamed they could have such influence, and they simply were not ready for it to end. Their hopes and dreams in the Baptist had grown each time they heard him preach about the coming kingdom. They could picture themselves with important positions in that kingdom. They could not give that up so quickly.

They also had grown to respect the Baptist more than any other man. Never had they known anyone so free from the fear of man, so confident, and so focused on his mission. The power of his vision and resolve swept up even the most learned and powerful into a new and living hope in the God of Israel.

The disciples who were with him day after day also witnessed a harmony in unfolding events. It was apparent that the very hand of God ruled his every move. Their days were filled with awe and wonder. These disciples could not joyfully embrace the possibility that something so wonderful and obviously ordained by God could come to an end so soon.

John and Andrew had never been very close to each other, but they had both become very close to the Baptist. Now, as they were obviously both thinking similar things about the events of the day, they turned to talk to each other.

"What are you thinking, my brother?" Andrew began.

"Could this possibly be the very Son of God? If so, this is the most important day of our lives, and nothing should keep us from finding and following Him."

"I have been thinking the same thing. But how can we find Him? Do you think John knows where He is? Do you think that we can even approach Him? John said He had come in humility like a lamb. There is something now burning in me to get to know Him. John said that this was what we were doing everything for, to prepare for the One who was coming. Once He has come, can we go on preparing for Him? Isn't it time to follow Him?"

"Yes. I feel the same way. We must ask John to help us find Him. If there is One who is so great that even John said he was unworthy to tie His sandals, how can we not follow Him? Maybe He will let us serve Him like we have the Baptist? What greater thing could a man do than to serve the Messiah?"

"No doubt that would be the greatest thing we could ever do. However, our dear friends here all seem to feel lost and discouraged. Being with the Baptist has been more wonderful than anything I ever dreamed of experiencing in my life. This has been like living the Scriptures of old. Even so, if what John is saying is true, we must go and find the One for whom we have dedicated ourselves in preparing the way. I do not want to be presumptuous, but how can we rest if One who is even greater than John is close by, much less the very Son of God Himself, whatever that may mean? We must find Him and try to become His disciples or His servants. Is this not what John trained us for?"

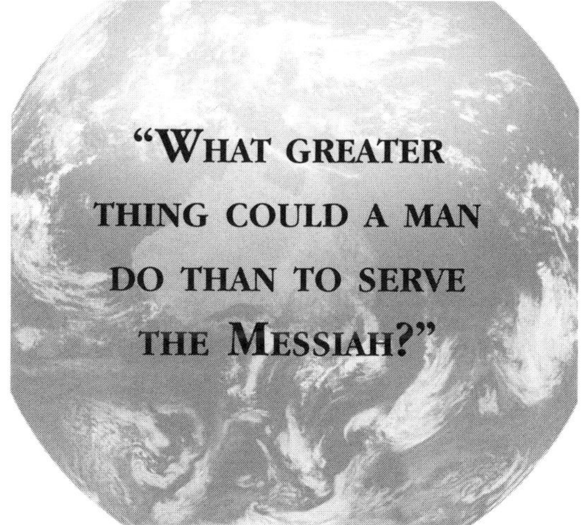

"We will have to ask the Baptist about all of this as soon as he returns from prayer. I know I will not be able to sleep until we know more about this Man. To think that we may have seen the Messiah today! I must admit, it is difficult to actually think that He is the Son of God, and that He existed before, as John said. We have seen marvelous things though, which can only be explained as coming from God. I do not believe that John would overstate who this is we have been trying to prepare the way for. For John, the most righteous man I have ever known, to say that he is not worthy to even untie His shoes..."

THE HEAVENLY REALMS WERE STIRRED LIKE THEY HAD NOT WITNESSED BEFORE. ALL OF HEAVEN AND HELL SEEMED TO BE MOBILIZING.

The angels who were guarding the encampment listened intently. They felt like the two disciples. They badly wanted to understand the events they had witnessed this day. The Holy One Himself had come to this little band. Heaven had opened and the Holy Spirit descended like they had never seen Him do before. The heavenly realms were stirred like they had not witnessed before. All of heaven and hell seemed to be mobilizing.

A great angelic warrior appeared in their midst. They lifted up their swords at once, and bowed low to salute him. The campfires all around suddenly blew with the wind that was stirred by his arrival. The great angel turned and bowed a salute to the disciples, who were now shifting their cloaks to cover themselves from the wind this great angel's presence had stirred. The great angel then turned to the commander of the company of angels who surrounded their camp.

"Tell me," he asked of the commander, "How did these do today?"

"They know of the Holy One," the commander replied, "but they do not understand Him. They are actually discouraged by what happened today, except for those two over there."

"Yes, I know of them," the great warrior replied. "They will follow the Holy One. They are heirs. Because of their calling they will soon become known to the evil one. Therefore, two who are of greater rank than I will come to guard them. They will post their own warriors and messengers so that you will be relieved of their care. There are many others who will also be coming to take their positions with some of these people. The time has finally come. The battle is about to begin. You have done very well to keep them until now, but it is now time for you to be relieved."

"Sir," the commander of the band interjected. "If I have done well, may I remain with you or be assigned to one of those who will join these disciples? Since we entered the realm of time, we have been in many battles, but the wonder of this is greater than anything we have known. We just cannot bear to think of leaving now. What we are seeing take place here is making all of the battles we have been through seem worth it," the commander replied.

The great angel's gaze intently surveyed this company of warriors. "Your request will be considered. You are a good and faithful commander, and would do well in the battles ahead. However, there are some things of great importance that I must inform you about that will be hard for you or your warriors to understand."

"Please tell me sir," the commander entreated.

"The evil one is intent on just one thing now—destroying the Holy One and His elect. Since he was foiled with his scheme to use Herod to do this he has been in a great rage. Very soon the dark one himself will appear to tempt the Holy One. We have been instructed to let him do it. I do not think he will succeed. He will then become even more enraged and he will try to kill the Baptist. You must let him do it."

"What?!" gasped the commander.

"Yes. You must let the evil one kill the Baptist."

"Why? Even the great ones say the Baptist has been one of the most faithful men that we have ever been given charge over. We were all sure that he would be taken up in the chariot like the prophet Elijah or even be translated like Enoch. Sir, please forgive me, but I must be sure about these orders."

"Yes, you heard me correctly. And I do understand what you are thinking, but do not fear. This is a victory for him and for us. Today the Baptist finished his course. He has done everything that he was given to do. Of all of the prophets, he has been the greatest. Even so, the elect are here now, though still unknown. The Baptist was the greatest of servants, but these are the heirs. The Baptist is as faithful as any man has yet been to his calling, but even he will not understand what is about to take place. He is from a different time than they are."

"THE EVIL ONE IS INTENT ON JUST ONE THING NOW— DESTROYING THE HOLY ONE AND HIS ELECT."

"But your excellency! I do not mean to question orders, but must we let the evil one kill him? Can he not be taken with more honor than that?"

"I do not understand all of these things myself. But I have watched many prophets and righteous men killed by the evil one. His power of darkness is great, but it is limited. Every time he uses his power to kill a righteous one, he is weakened for a time, and it allows many others to behold the light of truth. In fact, I have been told by those above me that many of the heirs are to be killed by him also."

THE WILLINGNESS OF THESE HOLY ONES TO SUFFER AT THE HANDS OF THE EVIL ONE WILL BE WHAT UTTERLY DEFEATS HIM.

"Your excellency! This is very hard to accept. Could we possibly stand by while he kills the heirs? This does not seem possible!"

"I'm sure we will be told more if we need to understand more. The Father's ways on this earth are a great mystery to us. Things are very different here. He only assures us that in the end we will all understand. None of us seem to understand the purpose for this yet, except for the Father and the Son. We have been told that it is because the heirs will love the truth more than they love their lives, and that their willingness to die at the hands of the evil one will work to weaken him. In the end, even one of your company will be able to bind him."

"Sir, I am a veteran of many battles, and though I know what you are saying must be true, it is still very hard to accept. I, too, have seen it weaken demons when they wound or kill a righteous one. In fact, I have witnessed that the more light one has who suffers their attacks, the more it weakens the evil ones who attack them. But are not the heirs called to retake this world from the evil one, and rule over it with the Son?"

"That is correct," the great warrior angel responded. "But somehow they will retake this world by their sufferings. In this way, they will prove their devotion to our God, and it will so weaken the evil one to attack those with such great light, that in the end even the lowest of the angelic ranks will subdue him. He will expend himself in wrath against them. There will be very many righteous ones who are allowed to suffer this way, and they will walk in far more light than we have yet seen in men. The willingness of these holy ones to suffer at the hands of the evil one will be what utterly defeats him. We have been given this knowledge because the time will come when many of us will have to let those we have been given the charge to protect, fall into the hands of the dark ones."

"I just cannot understand how the Holy One could allow this to happen," the commander wondered out loud. "We know He is here like a man to take back what Adam lost. How is it that He will allow the evil one to continue killing His own righteous ones after He has retaken authority over the world? Why would He then allow His fellow heirs to fall before the evil one? Why will He then not allow us to fight the evil hordes? The battle would be great, but we can easily defeat them, and these would not have to suffer."

"This is still a great mystery," the mighty messenger continued. "The ways of the Almighty are far beyond our ability to comprehend at times, but we know He is always wise and righteous. We were told that the heirs are to have this 'honor' of dying for the truth. By this they are proving their faithfulness. I admit whenever a prophet or righteous man has suffered in this way for not compromising the truth, I have been filled with awe and respect for them. I have also witnessed even the great commanders of the evil one not being able to restrain their own respect for them when they do this, as much as they might try to hide it. It is a marvelous thing to behold."

They stood together looking over the little band of men with obvious wonder and affection. The great angel then continued, speaking loud enough for the whole band of warriors to hear.

WE WERE TOLD THAT THE HEIRS ARE TO HAVE THIS 'HONOR' OF DYING FOR THE TRUTH. BY THIS THEY ARE PROVING THEIR FAITHFULNESS.

"Those who are weak and confused for most of their lives, can also love the truth and the Holy One more than they love their lives. When you see this, you will begin to understand how some of them may even rise to become heirs with the Holy One. As difficult as it is to understand many things that take place here, the courage and faithfulness of these who are so weak, standing at times resisting the evil one himself, is one of the great marvels we have been honored to behold. The entire host of heaven envies our commission. Even those on the far galaxies spend most of their time inquiring about the things in which we have been chosen to see and participate."

"You are right, sir," replied the commander, saluting his superior who was obviously about to leave. "I would not trade my place here for even the highest order of authority anywhere else. Thank you for this great trust."

THE HEAVENS WERE NOW SO STIRRED THAT THERE WAS AN ALMOST CONTINUOUS PASSING OF BOTH ANGELIC AND DEMONIC MESSENGERS.

"You would not be here if you had not earned it with your own faithfulness. I will pass on your request to stay."

As the great warrior departed, all of the angelic soldiers raised their swords in a salute. They had been allowed to hear what their commander had been told. They had already increased their vigilance watching over the disciples, knowing that some of them were of the elect. Now, because they had heard that the evil one would himself come to test the Holy One, they would be even more alert.

The heavens were now so stirred that there was an almost continuous passing of both angelic and demonic messengers. Angels of great power would at times light up the entire sky with their brilliance. Great winds, even storms, were stirred up on the earth as they passed.

"The mobilization has begun," said the commander to his company.

The spectacle grew until his soldiers soon forgot about their own recent visit from such a great warrior. At the same time, the disciples began to seek shelter from the wind and impending storms. The company of angels followed them closely.

Suddenly two great angelic captains with their thousands appeared before the little company guarding the disciples of the Baptist. They stepped up to the commander who bowed low before them. The company of warrior angels all raised their swords high while bowing on one knee. The captains acknowledged their salute with a nod, and then asked the commander to stand.

"We have come to assume responsibility for two of these disciples, John and Andrew," one of them said.

"They are the ones still talking over there. They have not slept and the light of the Spirit of truth has been upon them," the commander replied.

As the captains turned to see them, they drew their swords and bowed low to the ground, as the entire host that was with them did the same. The commander and his company stood by awkwardly.

When the captains arose, they turned back to the commander and said,

"Well done, commander. We relieve you of your duty to these two. Over the next few years many of these other disciples will also be commissioned, and then other captains will come for them."

"I understand," replied the commander.

Then the two angelic captains turned to John the Baptist, who was now standing nearby, looking at John and Andrew.

"The Holy Spirit has told him about these two. Tomorrow He will direct them to follow the Holy One. These will be the first. Their destiny is great. The mystery of God is about to be revealed. Permission has been granted for you to stay on the earth. For now you must stay with John and the other disciples until relieved and given another assignment."

"Thank you, sir. Please thank the captain of our host for me."

"You can thank him yourself. You will see him soon."

"Michael is coming here?"

"No. He has been here for many years. He is cloaked with humility like his Master," said one of the captains.

"He's the messenger who stays with the Holy One!" the commander exclaimed. "We had no idea that he was the captain!"

"Yes. That is him. You did not know him because he did not want you to. He did not want to draw any attention to the Holy One. If anyone would have known that he was here, it would have drawn attention that we did not yet want for the One he has been charged to watch over."

"He is very well cloaked. I actually talked with him today and had no idea."

"You will see him again tomorrow. He will trust you with other important matters because you have been found trustworthy. You will need to know them for your future assignment."

"Do you know my future assignment?" the commander inquired.

"I know something about it. You will help a man who is now a young Pharisee. He is one of the elect and will one day be as resolute as the Baptist. I do not know anything else about him, but I know if you are being assigned to him, he is a man with a great mission. You are now a warrior of renown among the hosts. Those to whom you are assigned will be those with a great mission."

John and Andrew did not sleep at all that night as if they perceived the stirring in the heavens that was taking place all around them. Both had determined they would do all that they could to find the One whom the Baptist had called "the Son of God."

"THAT'S HIM," THE BAPTIST ALMOST WHISPERED. "BEHOLD, THE LAMB OF GOD WHO TAKES AWAY THE SINS OF THE WORLD."

The next morning the disciples talked very little as they ate their bread. Crowds were already forming to hear the Baptist. None of them wanted to believe John's words, that his time was now up, and they were all hoping that the new day would bring the old John back. Then he appeared, as usual, about an hour after dawn.

The Baptist did not go down to the bank and begin preaching as he usually did. He just sat on a rock and looked over the crowds without saying anything. He then called John and Andrew and told them to stand beside him. He did not say anything to them for nearly ten minutes. Finally, both disciples were about to begin their barrage of questions when the Baptist stood to his feet, looking intently at a man who was walking alone by the bank.

"That's Him," the Baptist almost whispered. "Behold, the Lamb of God who takes away the sins of the world."

John and Andrew both began to breathe heavily. Their hearts were leaping within them.

"Is that the Man that you called 'the Son of God?'" John almost demanded as he studied Him.

"He is the One. Do what is in your heart to do," the Baptist continued, motioning for them to go.

The two disciples then did something they had never done before; they embraced the Baptist. His faint smile let them know that it was alright, maybe even appreciated. Then he nodded again toward the One he had called the Lamb.

Having seen the strange sight of the two disciples embracing John, the others gathered around him to ask what was happening.

"Where are those two going?"

"It is time for them to follow another," the Baptist answered.

The hearts of the disciples fell when they heard this. They had been a tight group and had been through much together. With all of the confusion from the day before, it was hard to see anyone leave their company. Even so, none of them spoke because they were surprised by the obvious joy that was on the face of the Baptist. Seldom had they seen him even smile; but now he was smiling broadly.

John discerned their thoughts and answered them just as if they had been thinking out loud.

"He is the Bridegroom. I am the friend of the Bridegroom. My joy is made complete just by seeing His joy. I have baptized you with water, but He is the One who will baptize you with the Holy Spirit and fire. He is the One I came to prepare the way for. He is the One whom all of the prophets came to prepare the way for. He existed from the beginning. Now He will take away the sin of the world."

They all stood and watched as Andrew and John approached Him. They were only a few paces behind Him, but did not seem to know what to do next. Then He turned and looked at them. The two disciples almost fell backwards. Their hearts were beating so hard that neither was able to say anything.

"What do you seek?" He asked.

Finally, John spoke up, "Rabbi, where do you dwell?"

Jesus smiled. "Come and you will see," He replied, motioning for them to join Him.

John and Andrew were beside themselves with joy and relief. They wanted to ask Him a thousand questions, but were determined to use discretion. Again John spoke up.

"We are disciples of the Baptist. He told us some things about you. Do you mind if we ask you some questions?"

"Please, be free," He answered.

I HAVE BAPTIZED YOU WITH WATER, BUT HE IS THE ONE WHO WILL BAPTIZE YOU WITH THE HOLY SPIRIT AND FIRE.

His tone was so calm, even friendly, that the disciples actually began to feel comfortable enough to talk freely with Him. Andrew then spoke up.

"Rabbi, we heard a voice yesterday when You were being baptized. We could not figure out who it came from. Last night the Baptist said that it was the voice of God..."

Jesus stopped and looked each of them in the eyes. The Baptist had penetrating eyes, but His were even more so. The two felt completely exposed as He gazed at them. For a moment they were very uncomfortable. He then reached out and put a hand on each of their shoulders to calm them.

"There are many things that I must tell you, but they would be hard for you to bear right now.

John was sent to prepare My way before Me, and he has done well. He has also prepared you well to follow Me. There are some things I will tell you, and there are some that you must receive directly from My Father. You will hear His voice again many times, both from within and without. I know you heard His voice, and I know you believe. Do not be afraid. To follow Me, your eyes and ears must be opened to things that you cannot now understand, but I will prepare you for them."

JESUS ALONE WOULD BE THE BRIDGE BETWEEN THE OLD AND THE NEW THAT WAS COMING.

The Baptist and his disciples were still watching as the three passed over the hill and out of sight. John somehow knew that it was the last time he would see Him. Even so, he was not sad. He wanted to follow Him, too, but had already been told that he could not. He was the last messenger of a Covenant, and Jesus alone would be the Bridge between the Old and the New that was coming. Soon the Baptist would join those of his order, all of those who had prepared the way for this day. How he longed to meet them! He longed to be a part of the great cloud of witnesses who had earned the right to watch all that was about to unfold on the earth. He also longed to see the Father and the great hosts of angels who attended Him, a few of whom he had briefly met in this life.

Now that John's task had been completed, he began to earnestly long for heaven. Even so, he was a servant. He determined to serve each day with all of his heart until his time came to depart. He looked at his disciples. He knew that many of them would one day follow the Lamb. He had to do all he could to prepare them for it.

The Baptist then turned and descended the hill to the bank of the Jordan, reciting the commandments of the Law with brief illustrations of how each was being broken by the people. He then recited the judgments that were promised for those who transgressed. He knew that they would never know they needed a Savior if they did not know God's righteousness, what He expected of His people, and how terribly they had failed Him. He was now even more resolved to make this clear to them.

With a voice that reached even the fringes of the multitude, his words cascaded down upon the people likes waves from the sea. Soon men were openly weeping and women were begging for mercy. His disciples took heart. Now, if possible, it seemed that he had even more fire than before. He did. From that day John had an even greater reason for his work. He had seen the King, and he had seen the heavens opened. The kingdom of heaven had come to earth, and was now walking among them.

Jesus shared His dwelling that night with John and Andrew. Encouraged that He seemed to genuinely enjoy their company, they talked to Him far into the night. He patiently listened to them, and answered their questions. By the time they laid down to sleep they felt as if they had known Him for a long time. They had. One day they would realize that they had known Him from the beginning. He was the One who stirred their hearts whenever the Scriptures were read. He was also the One who touched them with joy when they beheld the beauty of a sunset, or appreciated the grace and dignity of a righteous man or woman. All things had been made by Him and for Him, and in Him they were all held together. He was the Word of God, the communication from the Father to His creation, and the ultimate desire of that creation.

As tired as John was from not sleeping the night before, he had trouble sleeping again. As he looked at Jesus across the room, he could not believe his good fortune. He was now sure this was the Messiah. He was the coming King of Israel! Unlike Herod, He was the true King. Would He have mighty men to serve Him like David? Would they do exploits for Him like David's men had done for him? Would He be an even greater warrior than David? Yet, He was more patient and even more humble than anyone he had ever met. His sense of the glories that he was about to behold overwhelmed him. These were the days that the prophets had all spoken about, and he, John, the son of Zebedee, was privileged to be in the very center of them.

Andrew also lay awake for a long time with his thoughts. He pondered some of the answers Jesus had given them to their questions. He seldom answered their questions directly, but rather seemed to know what they really wanted to ask, but did not know how. He seemed to listen to their hearts rather than their words. Andrew then thought of his family, and Simon his brother. Jesus had told him and John that they needed to return to their families, and that He would find them later. He said He had to go into the wilderness for a time, alone, but He promised to come for them again. Though Andrew did not want to leave Him so soon after meeting Him, he could hardly wait to tell his family about the One they had found, especially Simon.

The two captains stood at the door of the little cottage. Their legions of angels were arrayed about them. Messenger angels were constantly passing by, but each would stop to salute the men in the cottage. The heavens were now opened. They now knew that the very fullness of the power of God dwelt in a Man. The One who spoke the universe into being now walked upon the dust of the earth. None of them had even dreamed they would see such things when they were assigned to the earth!

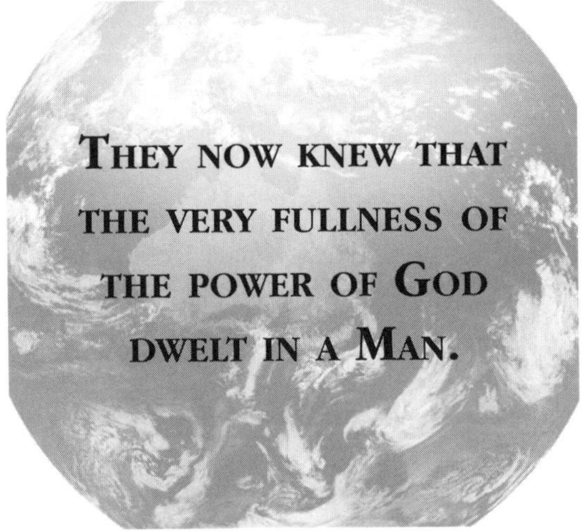

When the Son had left His place on the throne, all of the hosts of heaven marveled. When He entered the womb of the little girl, they were astonished. Angels watched over each star. Great ones watched over many stars and even galaxies. But there was not one angel in the universe now who would not trade his entire dominion to watch over a single man on earth. Men had taken on a whole new importance. They had now become the center of the universe.

"We have been on the earth since we were first assigned to guard the Tree of Life in the Garden," one of the captains said. "Now that Life walks as a Man. If any man knew who this was sleeping here..."

"Yes, but even the two here with Him do not really know. I have watched men for four thousand years now, since we drove the first two from the Garden. They have grown steadily in evil, just like the evil one. Their hearts and minds are continually set on evil. They have continued falling since the Garden. Now, even when they do good to one another, it is for selfish reasons. This has not happened anywhere else in the creation. I wonder constantly why the Almighty does not just destroy this little pocket of darkness. Instead, He sends His own Son! Even a speck of dust from this realm should not be allowed near Him, yet there He is, one of them!"

"The darkness in the hearts of men is getting greater," replied the other captain. "After being here for so long it is hard to understand how they will ever be brought back to the light. But here is the Light Himself, and we know nothing is impossible for Him. But how is He going to do it?"

The two captains bowed low to the ground as Michael stepped beside them. He was clothed as a messenger angel, but the captains recognized him immediately.

"I have been listening to you," Michael said, beckoning them to stand upright. "I understand very well what you think about this race of men. All of the evil in the universe has been concentrated here on this little speck of creation, this planet, and in these little creatures. Yet, there is a reason why the evil one has concentrated all of his power here. There is a destiny on man that is greater than any man has ever comprehended, or even those of us who have been here from the beginning have fully comprehended. The Almighty Himself intends to dwell here among them in the fullness of His glory. Men will one day be the eternal dwelling place of God."

The two captains gasped with astonishment at this statement.

"For the Son to come here was more than I have been able to understand," replied one of the captains, "but for the Almighty Himself to choose to dwell with them here, in His glory?!!!"

"Yes. There is a great capacity of men to do evil, but this is because there is a corresponding capacity for them to rise to the greatest heights of nobility and courage. They will actually be able to think, feel, and love the way the Father does."

"I have seen nobility in some men for brief periods," one of the captains said thoughtfully. "Enoch, Abraham, Moses, David, and a few others grew so great in the light that they did almost overcome the evil in their hearts. But there have been less than one in a million who even cared to know the God who made them. How will this entire race ever be made capable of seeing His glory, much less being His dwelling place?"

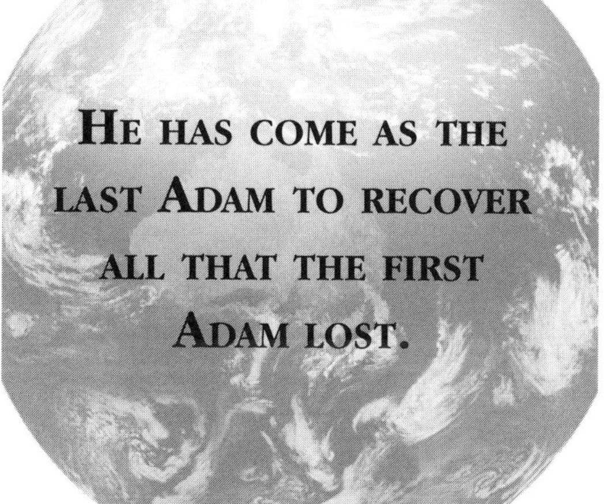

"It is beyond my own ability to understand as well," Michael admitted. "I just know that the Son is here to completely recover the earth. He will return it to the condition that we knew in the Garden. I was even instructed to now call Him 'the Son of Man,' instead of 'the Son of God.' He has come as the last Adam to recover all that the first Adam lost.

They fell silent for a time as they gazed at their King, sleeping. They looked at the other two who had been chosen to see His glory, and be His messengers. No angel in heaven was as foolish and weak as they were, yet here was the King sleeping beside them. Michael then continued.

THE LIGHT IN EVEN ONE OF HIS LITTLE ONES IS GREATER THAN ALL OF THE DARKNESS OF THE EVIL ONE.

"The first Adam walked where there was only good, but turned to evil. This One will walk where there is only evil, but will only do good. He will reveal the light of life to men, and they will begin to come out of the darkness. There will only be a few at first, but as the darkness continues to grow in mankind, so will the light from this time forth. Many will follow Him back to the love of the Father. These are the elect. In time the elect will prevail, and many will be saved from the darkness because of their witness. One day, because of these who are now weak and foolish, the whole creation will forever know true strength, that the light is greater than the darkness."

"If the light can prevail here, no one in heaven or any other realm will ever question that," one of the captains agreed. "Even the darkest, evil lords cannot get much more evil than we now see here."

"I wish that were so. It will get darker," Michael replied. "The fall is not yet complete, and it must be allowed to run its full course. Just as the Son has now manifested Himself in man, so will the evil one do the same. The evil seed that he sowed in man will fully mature in time. Then the earth will be even darker than this, but the light that the Son has brought to His own will stand against it and prevail. The light in even one of His little ones is greater than all of the darkness of the evil one. It is hard to understand all of this now, but I have seen the prophecies given to men as an oath from God, so it is sure.

"I am telling you this now captains because it will appear at times like the light has been defeated. You must never despair, regardless of how it appears to go here. The greatest courage is always revealed when it appears that defeat is inevitable. There are many mysteries that we cannot now understand, but we will later. Only remember that the Father has Himself given His word to men that it will be so that truth will prevail. For this reason we can be sure." ■

MorningStar Fellowship of Ministries

The MorningStar Fellowship of Ministries (**MFM**) was established to equip, oversee, and support ministries that are devoted to seeing radical, biblical Christianity preached, established, and lived on the earth. If you are seeking fellowship with others who are committed to doing all things for the sake of the gospel, to stand against the great darkness of our times, refusing to retreat and determined to advance for the sake of the light and truth that is found only in Jesus Christ, **MFM may be for you.**

For additional information or to request an application, contact:

MorningStar Fellowship of Ministries P.O. Box 19409
Charlotte, NC 28219 • (704) 522-8111, ext. 7
www.morningstarministries.org

MorningStar Fellowship of Churches

The MorningStar Fellowship of Churches **(MFC)** has been established as a fellowship of churches with a common destiny to prepare the church for the challenges of our generation. If you identify with MorningStar's vision, MFC may be for you and your congregation. Membership applications are now available.

For additional information or to request an application, contact:

MorningStar Fellowship of Churches P.O. Box 19409
Charlotte, NC 28219 • (704) 522-8111, ext. 7
www.morningstarministries.org

MFM Directory

The MorningStar Fellowship of Ministries

The MorningStar Fellowship of Ministries (MFM) was founded to serve three basic parts of the overall vision of MorningStar. First is the equipping, oversight, and support of ministries related to MorningStar. The second is to use the relationship that MorningStar has with many different parts of the body of Christ to promote interchange, understanding, and friendship between them. The third is for the mobilization of spiritual forces for the sake of the gospel. Current members of MFM are listed below. For more information or an application, please call our office at (704) 522-8111 ext. 7.

CANADA

Dean Downey, Pastor
Vineyard House
119 Rene Emard Rd.
Ile Perrot, Quebec J7V 8VS, Canada
(514) 425-0523
E-mail: mattedowney@yahoo.com

Sylvain Gauthier
Najoth Ministries
784 RR 7, Ste-Clothilde,
Quebec G0N 1C0, Canada
(418) 484-5611 / Fax: (418) 484-6611
E-mail: najoth@globetrotter.net

Rick Melvin
KATARTIZO
624 16th St. South
Lethbridge, Alberta T1J 3B2, Canada
(403) 328-7948 / Fax: (403) 329-3223
E-mail: rmelvin@agt.net

Bryan Yager
River of Life—Eagleview Ministries
205 Meadowbrook Rd.
Victoria, British Columbia V9E 1J5, Canada
(250) 479-7166 / Fax: (250) 479-7168
E-mail: Rolem@shaw.ca`

OTHER COUNTRIES

Dr. Francis Agbana
Life Builders International Network
P.O. Box 23808, London SE, 15 1ZL England, UK **and** P.O. Box 307, Lome
Republic of Togo, West Africa
E-mail: nationsowner@yahoo.com

K.V. Daniel
Voice of God Ministries International
Cemetery Road, Missions Quarters
Trichur—680001
Kerala, India

George Ferrar
Living Waters Ministries
Back Street, Caye Caulker
Belize, Central America
231-946-5622
E-mail: gferrar@btl.net

Teresa Hines
Glory to God Ministries
Andromeda Hill, 68 Yehuda Hayamit
StreetEntrance 3/ Apartment 3
Old Jaffa, ISRAEL 60138
E-mail: glorytwelve@aol.com

Andreas Keller (Pastor)
Stiftung Schleife
Pflanzschulstrasse 17, Postfach 75
CH-8411 Winterthur, Switzerland
+41 (052) 233-6080 / Fax: +41 (052) 233-6082
E-mail: office@schleife.ch

Jerry McNally (Pastor)
Living Hope International
Apdo 2-57, CP 72131, Puebla, MEXICO
Phone / Fax: +52 222-285-1419
E-mail: Jerry@TheCityofHope.org
Website: www.thecityofhope.org/
www.naciones.org.mx

Michael Quinn
Resurrection Life Ministries
1050 Rigg A/K 542 Latvia
+ 371-977-6548
E-mail: Michaelicu@aol.com

Ferry Wieland (Pastor)
Christian Fellowship Drachten
Trilker 3, 9222 MB Drachster Compagnie
Netherlands
+ 31 (51) 234-1095
E-mail: cfd@hiscfd.com
Website: www.hiscfd.com

UNITED STATES

ALABAMA

Miles Wylie Albright
Day's Dawn Ministries
245 C.R. 1595, Baileyton, AL 35019
(256) 796-2333

Ernest E. Brown (Pastor)
The Christian Center
9105 Alabama Highway 69, Arab, AL 35016
(256) 753-2237 / Fax: (256) 582-9889
E-mail: erniebrown@juno.com

Tracy Shellhorn
Manifest Ministries
PO Box 382227, Birmingham, AL 35242
(205) 980-4996
E-mail: atschell@bellsouth.net
Website: www.manifestministries.com

ARIZONA

Cory McClure (Pastor)
LifeWay Christian Fellowship
296 E. Frances Lane, Gilbert, AZ 85296
(480) 892-4522
E-mail: corym@lifewayfellowship.org
Website: www.lifewayfellowship.org

ARKANSAS

Randy Moser (Pastor)
The Gatherings
87 Nieboer Drive, Mountain Home, AR 72653
(870) 491-5299
E-mail: moserbunch@centurytel.net

CALIFORNIA

Kim Andersson (Pastor)
Christ the Rock Fellowship
2218 Ferry #C, Anderson, CA 96007
(530) 365-5048
E-mail: christtherock@c-zone.net
Website: www.christ_the_rock.org

Josh Dehmlow (Pastor)
InnerMission
2142 North Wilson Avenue, Fresno, CA 93704
(559) 222-7509
E-mail: dehmlow@attbi.com

H. Daniel Hanselman
House of Restoration
PO Box 142, Joshua Tree, CA 92252
(760) 366-2147 / Fax: (760) 366-3397
Email: familyrestoration@earthlink.net

COLORADO

Rich & Gail Harris (Pastors)
Living Word Fellowship/ Golden Eagle School of Practical Ministry
Mailing address only:26741 Hilltop Road, Evergreen, CO 80439
Phone/Fax: (303) 670-2208
E-mail: LWMISOS@cs.com

CONNECTICUT

Russell Leitch
Spirit Builders
16 Glenview Drive, Cromwell, CT 06416
Phone/Fax: (860) 635-2910
E-mail: spiritbuilders@juno.com

DISTRICT OF COLUMBIA

Wade Taylor
PO Box 15292, Washington, D.C. 20003-0292
(202) 365-1685
E-mail: wetbanner1@aol.com
Website: www.wadetaylor.net

FLORIDA

Steve Cruz
Good News Fellowship Church
201 SW 38th Avenue, Ft. Lauderdale, FL 33312
(954) 581-1612 / Fax: (954) 581-5617
E-mail: stevecruz@bellsouth.net

Randal Cutter (Pastor)
New Dawn Community Church
11030 Wiles Road, Coral Springs, FL 33076
(954) 753-7729 / Fax: (954) 345-2562
E-mail: NewDawn@NewDawn.org
Website: www.newdawn.org

Andrew DeLong (Pastor)
Tree of Life Church
2132 Shadowlawn Drive, Naples, FL 34112
(239) 530-2200 / Fax: (239) 530-2203
Website: www.tree-of-lfe-church.org

MFM Directory

Aaron Evans
Bridge Builders International Prophetic Ministries
PO Box 5057, Winter Park, FL 32793
(407) 681-2561 / Fax: (407) 681-0271
E-mail: bbimanager@aol.com
Website: www.bridgebuildersintl.org

David Hartz (Pastor)
Agape Life Church
3487 Hyde Park, Tallahassee, FL 32308
(850) 893-3032 / Fax: (850) 893-0658
E-mail: davidh246@aol.com

Jean LaCour
NET Training Institute
PO Box 536875, Orlando, FL 32853
(407) 236-9400 / Fax: (407) 849-1120
E-mail: nti@netinstitute.net
Website: www.netinstitute.net

Debra Nesgoda
Front Line Word Ministries, Inc.
803 South Lois Avenue, Tampa, FL 33609
(813) 286-0929 / Fax: (813) 286-9798
Cell: (813) 857-3865
E-mail: Debranesgoda@aol.com

Reggie Parker
Mighty Warriors Prophetic Ministries
1333 Don Carlos Trail, Deltona, FL 32725
(386) 575-2855

John Powell (Pastor)
Narrow Way Ministries
1949 Oak Water Drive, Jacksonville, FL 32225
(904) 928-1128
Email: jpowell133@aol.com

Greg Pusateri (Pastor)
Grace Community Fellowship
PO Box 1072, Starke, FL 32091
(904) 964-7208
E-mail: gracecf@atlantic.net
Website: www.gracecommunityfellowship.com

John Salmon (Pastor)
Gateway Community Church
PO Box 11874, Daytona Beach, FL 32120
(386) 274-2733 / Fax: (386) 253-3859
E-mail: lifeshapers@cs.com

Linda Spaulding
Levite Ministry
1224 Maple Street, Lakeland, FL 33810
(863) 858-5883
E-mail: Linda@LeviteMinistry.com
Website: www.Leviteministry.com

Rick & Bette Strombeck
Koinonia Ministries
705 East Pine Street, Orlando, FL 32801
(407) 291-3305 / Fax: (407) 422-9133
E-mail: rbstrombeck@bellsouth.net

Bill Taylor
25167 Rosamond Ct., Punta Gorda, FL 33983
(941) 629-2286

Keith Upchurch (Pastor)
Liberty Ministries and Fellowship & God's House
210 N. Lakeshore Way, Lake Alfred, FL 33850
Mailing Address: PO Box 252,
Lake Alfred, FL 33850
(863) 299-7936 / E-mail: klupchurch@juno.com

Craig Wendel (Pastor)
Tree of Life Church
2132 Shadowlawn Drive, Naples, FL 34112
(239) 530-2200 / Fax: (239) 530-2203
E-mail: stalkinggod@earthlink.net
Website: www.tree-of-life-church.org

GEORGIA

John Enlow (Pastor)
Refuge to the Nations
3617 Nina Court, Loganville, GA 30052
(770) 554-2131
E-mail: johnenlow@mindspring.com
Website: www.refugetothenations.com

Ray Kiertekles
Restoration Life Ministries
4989 Peachtree Parkway, Suwanee, GA 30024
678-969-3379 / Fax:678-947-1904
Email: RLMRSK@aol.com

Marc Lawson (Pastor)
Church at North Gate
4923 Canton Rd, Marietta, GA 30066
Mailing Address: PO Box 2190,
Woodstock, GA 30188
(678) 494-2193 / Fax: (770) 592-0858
E-mail: info@churchatnorthgate.com
Website: www.churchatnorthgate.com

Ryan Lawson (Pastor)
Church at North Gate
PO Box 2190, Woodstock, GA 30188
(678) 494-2193
E-mail: rlawson@ngla.org
Website: www.ngla.org

Barry Perez
New Covenant Church of Thomasville
48 Patterson Still Spur E.
Thomasville, GA 31757
(229) 226-3246 / (229) 226-3243

Keith Smith (Pastor)
Keith Smith Ministries, Inc.
Providence Church
(912) 530-7771
www.providenceoutreachministries.org

HAWAII

Karen Nicoli
Good News Fellowship Ministries
140 Uwapo Road, # 28102, Kihei, HI 96753
(808) 874-3652 / E-mail: Kearny77@aol.com

IDAHO

David McClellan (Pastor)
Community Christian Center /
Strong Tower Ministries
4698 N. Tattenham Way, Boise, ID 83713
(208) 939-5155
Website: www.communitychristiancenter.com

Eric Swisher
All About Him Worship Center
6198 South 46th East, Idaho Falls, ID 83406
(208) 529-0098 / E-mail: ens@onewest.net

ILLINOIS

Georganne Schweickert
Knowing Him Ministries
1419 Woodhill Drive, Northbrook, IL 60062
(847) 498-3628

Tony Danhelka
Riverwoods Christian Center
35 W 701 Riverwoods Lane, St Charles, IL 60174
(630) 584-2222, ext. 207 / Fax: (630) 443-0286
E-mail: tonydanhelka@sbcglobal.net
Website: www.riverwoodschristiancenter.org

Theresa Frerichs (Pastor)
Praise Ministries Church & Ministry Training Center
329 Stevens Street, Geneva, IL 60134
Phone / Fax: (630) 208-7818
E-mail: praiseminister@aol.com

Hilton Thomas
3377 Maple Tree Lane, Wadsworth, IL 60083
(874) 244-0519 / Fax: (874) 244-1446
E-mail: Hilton.Thomas@att.net

Robert Whitt (Pastor)
Family Life Church
1216 St. Charles Street, Elgin, IL 60123
(847) 717-4878 / Fax: (847) 697-4987
E-mail: familylifechurch@ameritech.net
Website: www.familylifechurch.com

INDIANA

Bob Combs
3605 Poinsettia Drive, Indianapolis, IN 46227
(317) 881-1949 / Email: letspray@es4.com

Doug Kimball
PO Box 473, Galveston, IN 46932
(574) 699-6184 /
E-mail: dougandkay@verison.net

Bill NeSmith
Harvest Light Ministries
6094 Prairie Stream Way, Columbus, IN 47203
(812) 372-9444
E-mail: Bill@harvestlm.org
Website: www.harvestlm.org

Garry Dean Vermilion (Pastor)
The Rock
3443 S. Lincoln Blvd., Marion, IN 46953
765-664-2281 / garydean3@yahoo.com

H. Dean Wollard (Pastor)
Church of the Cornerstone
PO Box 743, Auburn, IN 46706
(260) 925-4360
Website: www.geocities.com/cornerstone_world_outreach

IOWA

Linda Schreurs
Intimacy with God Ministries
6829 River Bend Drive, Johnston, IA 50131
(515) 270-0231 / Fax: (515) 331-3066
E-mail: LMSchreurs@aol.com
Website: www.intimacy-with-god.com

MFM Directory

KANSAS

Nick A. Harris (Pastor)
One Heart Ministries
PO Box 883 or 9377 SW Pine Road,
Andover, KS 67002

Jerry & Ruth Wickline (Pastors)
Spirit Life Church, Int.
447 Eshelman Street, McPherson, KS 67460
Friday SOS: 251 North 10th Street, Salina, Kansas
Saturday SOS: 615 N. Main, Wichita, Kansas
Sunday, SOS: 505 S. Ridge Rd., Hesston, Kansas
(620) 241-3933 / E-mail: jrwickline@juno.com
Website: www.spiritlifeministries.net

KENTUCKY

Marion Fawns (Pastor)
Church of the Harvest
2450 Osborne Road, Mt. Sterling, KY 40353
Phone/Fax: (859) 498-7983
E-mail: cotharvest@aol.com

LOUISIANA

Meg Jones
1938 Ferndale Avenue, Baton Rouge, LA 70808
(225) 383-5820
E-mail: Rosedoor@aol.com

MAINE

John Connor
16 Summer Street, Winthrop, ME 04364
(207) 377-2015 / E-mail: jconnor@ctel.net

MARYLAND

Brian Eichelberger
15726 Pointer Ridge Drive, Bowie, MD 20716
(301) 390-7926 / E-mail: brian@ioip.com

John Metcalfe
4605 Olden Court, Bowie, MD 20715
(410) 721-1619 / E-mail: jmet_2000@yahoo.com

MASSACHUSETTS

Tom Dobrient
456 Phinney's Lane, Centerville, MA 02632
(508) 778-4355 / Fax: (508) 778-6564
E-mail: Dobrient@cape.com

Barry Grauman (Pastor)
Taconic Valley Christian Fellowship
3399 Hancock Road, Williamstown, MA 01267
(413) 738-5814
E-mail: TaconicVCF@aol.com

Donna Milham
Eagle & Dove Ministries
954 Washington St. Gloucester, MA 01930
(978) 283-9076 / Fax: (978) 283-8776
E-mail: dmilham@cove.com
Website: www.eagledove.com

MISSOURI

Michael Banes (Pastor)
Bykota Church
PO Box 535, Carthage, MO 64836
(417) 358-3991 / Fax: (417) 358-7876
E-mail: mbanes@bykotachurch.org

MONTANA

Thomas (Tom) C. Banks (Pastor)
International Church of Helena, Montana, (ICHM)
609 S. Harris, Helena, MT 59601
(406) 443-1191 / (406)-439-6938
Email: ptbanks@juno.com

Albert LaRance (Pastor)
Morning Star House of Prayer
PO Box 1420, Lame Deer, MT 59043
(406) 477-6612 / Fax: (406) 477-6635
E-mail: getncontact@mshop.org
Website: www.mshopchurch.org

Lloyd C. Phillips (Pastor)
FLINT Net (Fellow Laborers' Intl. Network)
PO Box 113, Missousla, MT 59806
(406) 251-5730 / Fax: (406) 251-7035
E-mail: flintnet@flintnet.org
Website: www.flintnet.org

NEW JERSEY

Steve Burton (Pastor)
House of Praise Ministries
488 Monroeville Road, Woolwich, NJ 08085
(856) 467-0986
E-mail: Freedom8800@yahoo.com

Margaret Clark (Pastor)
The Gospel Fellowship
626 Plainsboro Road, Plainsboro, NJ 08536
(609) 799-5637 / Fax: (609) 799-0012
E-mail: gfipastor@juno.com

David & Evelyn Scull (Pastors)
Jubilee Living Word Ministries
PO Box 333, Quinton, NJ 08072
(856) 451-1356
E-mail: david_scull@comcast.net

Andrew Surace (Pastor)
Covenant Life Christian Fellowship
PO Box 1038, Marmora, NJ 08223
(609) 390-1999 / Fax: (609)390-3688
E-mail: Drew5Aces@aol.com

NEW YORK

Dylan Bowden (Pastor)
New Covenant Community Church
158 Windy Hill Roday, Greenwich, NY 12834
(518) 695-5534
Website: www.newcovenantcommunity.org

Gail Breden
The Word & Spirit Ministries
238 Wallkill Road, Walden, NY 12586
(845) 778-7086
E-mail: Gail_B@juno.com

Bob & Kathy Campbell (Pastors)
Harvest Fellowship
4647 Resevoir Road, Geneso, NY 14454
Phone/Fax: (585) 243-9280
E-mail: Bob@HFNC.org
Website: www.HFNC.org

Roy Esposito (Pastor)
Restoration Christian Fellowship
PO Box 1194, East Northport, NY 11731
(631) 261-0323
E-mail: restoration12@juno.com
Website: www.rdf-church.org

James Exner (Pastor)
Syracuse Airport Christian Fellowship/ Ministries
7744 Frontage Road Plaza, Cicero, NY 13039
(315) 458-4210 / Fax: (315) 699-9329
E-mail: sacf99@yahoo.com
Website: www.sacfm.org

Fred & Donna Hoover (Pastors)
Abide in the Vine Fellowship
1277 Taylor Road, Owego, NY 13827
(607) 687-3426 / Fax: (607) 687-0043
E-mail: thevine@spectra.net

Tom & Marianne Kapinos
Wings of the Father
141 Fernald Ave, Buffalo, NY 14218
Bus: (716) 824-2619 / Fax: (716) 824-7676
E-mail: mannonthecross@aol.com

Jim & Peg McLaughlin (Pastors)
New Beginnings Church
242 Dan Main Road, Norwich, NY 13815
Phone (607) 334-2833 / Fax:: (607) 334-3860
E-mail: jrmclaughlin@juno.com
Website: www.newbeginningsnorwich.org

Diane Scalchunes (Pastor)
Deep Waters Ministry
PO Box 2091, Port Washington, NY 11050
(576) 944-5015 / Fax: (516) 944-6879
E-mail: LK54@optonline.net
Website: www.deepwatersministry.com

Robert Seymour (Pastor)
Abide in the Vine Fellowship
1277 Taylor Road, Owego, NY 13827
(607) 687-3426 / Fax: (607) 687-0043
E-mail: berttoots@pronetisp.net

Gary Wallin (Pastor)
Restoration Christian Fellowship
96 Upper Sheep Pasture Road,
E. Setauket, NY 11733
(516) 941-4937
E-mail: pastorgary@rcf-church.com
Website: www.rcf-church.com

Deb Warner
Set Free Inc.
PO Box 245, Buffalo, NY 14215
(716) 553-3370
E-mail: dwarner@setfreeinc.org

NORTH CAROLINA

Pamela Ayres
Hanzel and Gretel Children's Ministry
P.O. Box 627, Moravian Falls, NC 28654
Phone: (336) 921-4467 / Fax: (336) 921-4468
E-mail: hesjoy777@hotmail.com

MFM Directory

Barbara Clark
267 Micah's Way, Moravian Falls, NC 28654
(336) 921-2996
E-mail: Biblebarb@aol.com

Bruce Corwin
Trinity Christian Prep School
6411 Sharon Road, Charlotte, NC 28210
(704) 554-0092 / Fax: (704) 552-6299
E-mail: btc@trinityprep.com
Website: www.trinitryprep.com

Earl & Sabrina Coulston
Accounts Ministry
PO Box 174, Pineville, NC 28134
(704) 543-7143 / Fax: (704) 544-2729
E-mail: Acoulston@aol.com

Trisha Doran
MorningStar Fellowship Church
PO Box 440, Wilkesboro, NC 28697
(336) 651-2400 / Fax: (336) 651-2430
Website: www.morningstarministries.org

Marla Filotei
Power in the Word Ministries, Int.
1326 Pearl Crescent Drive, Charlotte, NC 28216
(704) 392-2027
E-mail: Ephesians6@aol.com

Lucy Finch
PO Box 5692, High Point, NC 27262
Fax: (336)889-4862
E-mail: LucyPull@aol.com

Tom (Pastor) & Mary Anne Hardiman
MorningStar Fellowship Church
PO Box 440, Wilkesboro, NC 28697
(336) 651-2400 / Fax: (336) 651-2430
Website: www.morningstarministries.org

David Hart
MorningStar Fellowship Church
PO Box 440, Wilkesboro, NC 28697
(336) 651-2400 / Fax: (336) 651-2430
Website: www.morningstarministries.org

Carroll Henderson Jr. (Pastor)
Laurel Wood Ministries
124 Gamble Loop Road,
Bessemer City, NC 28016
Phone / Fax: (704) 629-0262
E-mail: jrscch@bellsouth.net

Jim Hill
His Heart Missions
PO Box 1742, Mooresville, NC 28115
E-mail: hisheartmissions@aol.com

Reggie & Debbie Hill
Helping Hands, Inc.
1241 Briar Creed Road, Charlotte, NC 28205
Phone / Fax: (704) 568-7905
E-mail: 1way2him@helpinghandsinc.org

John Holcomb
MorningStar Fellowship Church
PO Box 440, Wilkesboro, NC 28697
(336) 651-2400 / Fax: (336) 651-2430
Website: www.morningstarministries.org

Bobby & Ginger Hussey (Pastors)
MorningStar Fellowship Church
PO Box 440, Wilkesboro, NC 28697
(336) 651-2400 / Fax: (336) 651-2430
Website: www.morningstarministries.org

Leonard Jones
MorningStar Fellowship Church
PO Box 440, Wilkesboro, NC 28697
(336) 651-2400 / Fax: (336) 651-2430
Website: www.morningstarministries.org

Rick Joyner (Senior Pastor)
MorningStar Fellowship Church
PO Box 440, Wilkesboro, NC 28697
(336) 651-2400 / Fax: (336) 651-2430
Website: www.morningstarministries.org

Joel Killion (Pastor)
Inner Life Ministries
5880 Terriwood Drive, Rocky Mount, NC 27803
(252) 937-6726 / E-mail: joelkillion@yahoo.com
Website: www.innerlife.injesus.com

Steve Lappin (Pastor)
2014 Cardinal Loop, Stanley, NC 28164
(704) 822-2412 / Fax: (704) 822-2413
E-mail: steve@charlottebythelake.com
Website: charlottebythelake.com

Robin McMillian (Pastor)
MorningStar Fellowship Church
PO Box 440, Wilkesboro, NC 28697
(336) 651-2400 / Fax: (336) 651-2430
Website: www.morningstarministries.org

Brad McClendon (Pastor)
MorningStar Fellowship Church
PO Box 440, Wilkesboro, NC 28697
(336) 651-2400 / Fax: (336) 651-2430
Website: www.morningstarministries.org

Travis Newton
7235 Wingstone Lane, Charlotte, NC 28262
(704) 503-1086 / E-mail: JTN555@aol.com

Matt Peterson (Pastor)
MorningStar Fellowship Church
PO Box 440, Wilkesboro, NC 28697
(336) 651-2400 / Fax: (336) 651-2430
Website: www.morningstarministries.org

Nathan Plowman (Pastor)
MorningStar Fellowship Church
PO Box 440, Wilkesboro, NC 28697
(336) 651-2400 / Fax: (336) 651-2430
Website: www.morningstarministries.org

Carey & Suzanne Ramsey
Lovingkindness
690 Sink Road, Lexington, NC 27295
Phone/Fax: (336) 248-2215

Don Robertson
DREAM of Restoration Ministries
PO Box 300, Glendale Springs, NC 28629
(336) 982-3526 / Fax: (336) 982-3521
E-mail: phil211@skybest.com

Steven (Pastor) & Mindy Scroggs
Mountain Vintage Fellowship
3867 Sweeten Creek Road, Arden, NC 28704
(828) 687-9234
E-mail: Steve@mountainvintage.org

Alan Smith
Stony Point Christian Publications
PO Box 231, Stony Point, NC 28678
(704) 585-2355 / Fax: (704) 585-2302
Website: www.spchristianpub.org

Randy Strombeck
Koinonia Ministries
344 Knollwood Drive, Wilkesboro, NC 28697
(336) 838-6701 / Fax: (336) 838-6702
E-mail: cstrombeck@rivercto.net

Clifton Sutton (Pastor)
Just Like Jesus Ministries
PO Box 130, Burlington, NC 27216
(336) 538-0069 / Fax: (336) 584-0040
E-mail: clifds@earthlink.net

Steve Thompson (Pastor)
MorningStar Fellowship Church
PO Box 440, Wilkesboro, NC 28697
(336) 651-2400 / Fax: (336) 651-2430
Website: www.morningstarministries.org

Trevor Tiessen
MorningStar Fellowship Church
PO Box 440, Wilkesboro, NC 28697
(336) 651-2400 / Fax: (336) 651-2430
Website: www.morningstarministries.org

Rev. Jeanne Turner
Light of the World Ministries
267 Laurel Lane Apt. F, N. Wilkesboro, NC 28659
336-984-4417 / Fax 336-984-4418

David White
Harvest Now Ministries
PO Box 381, Moravian Falls, NC 28654
E-mail: harvestnow@earthlink.net

Byron Wicker (Pastor)
Calvary Community Church
(704) 644-3540 / Fax: (704)799-1928
E-mail: Bulrushes@msn.com
Website: www.hisharvest.org

Robert & Kathy Whitlow
Providence Ventures
6700 Providence Road, Charlotte, NC 28226
PROVVENINC@aol.com

Suzy Yaraei
MorningStar Fellowship Church
PO Box 440, Wilkesboro, NC 28697
(336) 651-2400 / Fax: (336) 651-2430
Website: www.morningstarministries.org

NORTH DAKOTA

Andrea Veach
301 7th Ave S.E., Rugby, ND 58368
(701) 776-5890

OHIO

Lois Hoshor (Pastor)
Soul Seekers Evangelistic Association
PO Box 547, Thornville, OH 43076-0547
(740) 246-6272 / Fax: (740) 246-6694
E-mail: soulseekers7@itilink.com

MFM Directory

David & Donna Kelly (Pastors)
Passion and Fire Worship Center
P.O. Box 145, West Chester, OH 45071-0145
(513) 777-8217 / Fax: (513) 777-8209
E-mail: pfworshipcenter@aol.com
Website: www.passionandfire.org

Hombre Liggett (Pastor)
Church of the Final Harvest
420 W. Third Street, Dover, OH 44622
(330) 343-1905
E-mail: jesus@harvestchurch.com
Website: www.harvestchurch.com

Tim Troyer (Pastor)
Berlin Christian Fellowship
PO Box 396, Berlin, OH 44610
(330) 893-3115 / Fax: (330) 893-3306
E-mail: bcf@tusco.net
Website: www.tusco.net/bcf

Barry (Pastor) & Tricia Tucker
ValleyView Church
410 North Main Street, Englewood, OH
Phone/Fax: (937) 836-3826
E-mail: Ezekiel362627@juno.com, trish.t@juno.com
Website: www.valleyviewchurch.net

David Turner (Pastor)
Hope Christian Assembly
451 Smith Road, Columbus, OH 43228
(814) 870-6180
E-mail: dturner91@yahoo.com
Website: www.turnerministries.com

OREGON

Ray Maestas
Harvest Rock Church
225 SW 1st Ave #8, Ontario, OR 97914
Phone: (541) 889-6625 / Fax: (541) 889-3915
E-mail: rgmaes@aol.com

James Moore
Pioneer Life Ministries
1057 Rural Avenue SE, Salem, OR 97302
Phone / Fax: (503) 371-7669
E-mail: fivefoldmin@yahoo.com

Jacob Ray
715 Parkmeadow Loop, Salem, OR 97303
(503) 390-2978 / (971) 240-0193
E-mail: windwords7@yahoo.com

Mark Stevens
Evening Light Ministries
330 Depot, Fairview, OR 97024

PENNSYLVANIA

Cynthia Brubaker (Pastor)
Glenside / Abington United Methodist Churches
412 E. Sentner Street, Philadelphia, PA 19120
(215) 535-4930
E-mail: randy.cindy@juno.com

Stanton Higley (Pastor)
New Life Fellowship World Outreach Center
PO Box 81, Rte. 646, Cyclone, PA 16726(814) 465-3272 / E-mail: srnjhigley@hotmail.com

Ted Moyer (Pastor)
Rock Community Church
PO Box 64225, Souderton, PA 18964
(215) 723-8678
E-mail: tmmoyer@entermail.net
www.rockthechurch.org

SOUTH CAROLINA

Jerry Ashley (Pastor)
Daystar Ministries
100 W. Richardson Avenue
Summerville, SC 29483
(843) 875-4370 / Fax: (843) 875-4341
E-mail: daystar@dycon.com

Terry Butler (Pastor)
New Covenant Praise Church
265 Wire Road, Aiken, SC 29801
(803) 642-5793 / Fax: (803) 648-9053
E-mail: tbutler265@msn.com
Website: www.newcovenantpraise.com

David Davenport
Shiloh Chapel
1860-B Cornish Ave., Charleston, SC 29412
(843) 332-2145 / E-mail: shilohchapel@aol.com

Rodger Martin

616 Lakeview Boulevard
Hartsville, SC 29550
(843) 332-0468
E-mail: rodgerdmartin@juno.com

Bill Perry (Pastor)

Hartsville Community Fellowship
PO Box 1739, Hartsville, SC 29551
(843) 383-8555 / Fax: (843) 383-0085
E-mail: HCF001@aol.com

Jeanne Turner

Light of the World Ministries
120 Ballentine Lane, Chapin, SC 29036
(803) 345-7482 / Fax: (803) 345-6148
E-mail: Light-of-the-world@juno.com

Dr. Samuel Tyler

Vanguard Foursquare Church
1650 West Blackstock Road,
Spartanburg, SC 29301
Mailing Address: PO Box 170008,
Spartanburg, SC 29301
(864) 574-2777 / Fax: (864) 574-0040
E-mail: vanguard@cfaith.com

TENNESSEE

Crispin A. & Rebecca D. Bennett

B & B Ministries
211 London Lane, Franklin, TN 37067
615-599-2425 / Fax: 877-437-2594
rythman@mail.com / beccab@mail.com

Derrek Bowman

120 East Central Avenue
LaFollette, TN 37766
(423) 566-4550
E-mail: derreksplace@comcast.net

Doug Floyd (Pastor)

Spring of Light
PO Box 421, Townsend, TN 37882
(423) 983-9015
E-mail: doug@springoflight.org
Website: www.springoflight.org

Scott MacLeod (Pastor)

Provision / Fortress Fellowship
1419 Clinton Street, Nashville, TN 37203
(615) 327-1200 / (615) 791-1181
E-mail: ScottMac7@lwol.com
Website: www.provisioninternational.org / www.zadokministries.org

Mike McClung (Pastor)

Lionheart Fellowship /
Greater Knoxville Area House of Prayer
2308 Alcoa Hwy, Alcoa, TN 37701
(865) 984-0302 / Fax: (865) 984-5809
E-mail: fellowship@lionheartministries.org
Website: www.lionheartministries.org/ www.knoxhop.org

Craig Schaub (Pastor)

Spirit of Life Church
3646 Murfreesboro Road, Antioch, TN 37013
Phone: (615) 641-5433 / Fax: (615) 641-5614
E-mail: office@renewedmind.com
Website: www.renewedmind.com

Susan Sillman Todd

7000 South York Hwy, Clarkrange, TN 38553
(931) 863-5113
E-mail: RSillman@aol.com

Darrell Simbeck (Pastor)

Ascension Life Fellowship
1510 Nova Street, Athens, TN 37303
(423) 745-7290
E-mail: Ascensionlife@aol.com

TEXAS

Tara Dorroh

At His Feet Ministries
18351 Kuykendahl #463, Spring, TX 77379
(281) 320-9637 / Fax: (281) 251-2979
Email: athisfeet@pdq.net
Website: www.athisfeetministries.org

David Fees (Pastor)

Christ Fellowship Ministries
#2 Westlane Place, Plano, TX 75074
(972) 516-9813
Email: dfees@attbi.com

MFM Directory

Carl & Kristy Greer
2201 N. Collins, Suite 156, Arlington, TX 76011
(817) 261-7137 / Fax: (817) 274-2776
E-mail: ckgreer@msn.com

Pat & Marlene Hodges (Pastors)
Spirit of Grace Church & Omega Ministries
PO Box 90173, Houston, TX 77290
(281) 355-8535
E-mail: SpiritofGrace@juno.com
Website: www.spiritofgrace.org

Doug O'Neal
635 Fawn Ridge #219, Dallas, TX 75224
(214) 438-3169
E-mail: douglasdeano@yahoo.com

UTAH

Tracee Anne Loosle
Intrepid Heart Ministry
854 N Dillon Drive, Ogden, Utah 84404
(801) 782-5663 / E-mail: firebride7@yahoo.com

VIRGINIA

Peggy Kannaday
411 23rd Street, Virginia Beach, VA 23451
(822) 783-3929 / Fax: (822) 784-1990
E-mail: peggy@uriel.net

WASHINGTON

Tom & Jackie Archer
25760 174th Place SE, Covington, WA 98042
(253) 638-8490 / E-mail: eagleeye37@aol.com

Symon Boschma
Highway of Life Ministries
2007 Hampton Road, Everson, WA 98247
Phone/Fax: (360) 354-1395
E-mail: Symon@w-link.net

Steve Denton
Come Together Now
9017 North Harborview Drive,
Gig Harbor, WA 98332
(253) 851-0737
E-mail: Steve@westerlymarine.com

Deborah Deonigi
PO Box 1140, Maple Valley, WA 98038
(425) 413-9118

Robert Foster (Pastor)
Whatcom County Prophetic Page/ My Father's House Fellowship
3324 Kelly Road, Bellingham, WA 98226
(360) 592-2531
E-mail: rfoster@fidalgo.net
Website: www.fidalgo.net/~rfoster.html

Angela Greenig (Pastor)
Setfree Ministries
Maple Lawn Elementary School
Sumner, WA 98390
(253) 863-8031
E-mail: me@sfministries.org
Website: www.sfministries.org

Lisa Kitchen
Aggressive Ministries
206 Frontage Road, North Suite A1
Algona, WA 98001
(253) 709-6441
E-mail: Gapline1@aol.com

Paul "Red" & Patricia Wilson (Pastors)
Aggressive Ministries
P.O. Box 731288, Puyallup, WA 98373
(253) 279-5763/Fax: (253) 862-1859
E-mail: aggressive@cfaith.com
Website: www.aggressiveministries.org

WEST VIRGINIA

Demetrius Apostolon
Body of Christ Ministries
506 Jefferson Avenue, Huntington, WV 25704
(304) 697-1977
E-mail: apostolond@msn.com

Terry Choate
Dare to Disciple
PO Box 607, Athens, WV 24712
E-mail: choatesrus@yahoo.com